GW00722496

THE SUCCESSFUL TREASURE HUNTER'S ESSENTIAL DOWSING MANUAL

How to Easily Develop Your Latent Skills to Find Treasure in Abundance

David Villanueva

Published by True Treasure Books
www.truetreasurebooks.com

Copyright © David Villanueva 2005

ISBN 0-9550325-0-4

ACKNOWLEDGEMENTS

Thanks for invaluable help to: Dowsers Jim Longton and Frank Delamere; Mike Scott who produced the illustrations and Bob Whalley, National Co-ordinator for Policy, National Council for Metal Detecting, for considerable assistance with the Treasure Act.

WEIGHTS AND MEASURES

Weights and Measurements used in this manual are largely metric as that is the current European standard. Unfortunately metric is not international and will be unfamiliar to some readers. In measurement of length: metres and yards can be assumed to be the same for our purposes. I have included a conversion table below:

Imperial to Metric		Metric to Imperial	
1 inch:	2.54 centimetres	1 centimetre:	0.39 inch
1 foot:	30.48 centimetres	1 metre:	3.28 feet
1 yard:	0.91 metre	1 metre:	1.09 yards
1 gram:	0.035 ounce	1 ounce:	28.35 grams
1 acre:	0.407 hectare	1 hectare:	2.47 acres
1 mile:	1.61 kilometres	1 kilometre:	0.62 mile

All rights reserved. Nothing may be reproduced from this work or stored in any form of information retrieval system without the express written permission of the publisher. The author and publisher issue this manual on the understanding that while every effort has been made to ensure the accuracy of all the information presented, no liability will be accepted for any loss or profit, direct or otherwise as a consequence of using any of the information presented. The opinions given are those of the author who is acting in good faith according to extensive research undertaken by him and who confirms that he himself uses the principles described.

CONTENTS

Page

Introduction...4

A Brief History of Dowsing...5

How Does Dowsing Work?...8

Finding and Using a Dowser..10

The Pendulum...11

The L-rod..15

Map Dowsing...24

Photographing Treasure Auras...26

Treasure Engineering...29

Research...33

Metal Detectors...36

Putting It All Together..40

Treasure Hunting Basics..45

National Council for Metal Detecting Code of Conduct....................46

Gaining Search Permission..47

Search Agreements...49

Living With The Treasure Act...51

Long-Range Locators...58

Bibliography & Further Information...59

INTRODUCTION

I started recreational treasure hunting over 30 years ago and enjoyed the hobby so much I dreamt of giving up my job so I could treasure hunt as often as I liked. The problem was that I couldn't find treasure quickly enough, so the burning question for me has always been: how can I find more treasure in less time? I read the books and the magazines and there is plenty of good advice. Buy the best equipment you can afford. Develop your skills. Research thoroughly. Good advice but is it enough? The majority of treasure locations are unknown and most finds are accidental. Or are they?

Reading through the treasure hunting magazines there are countless stories of finds being made in remarkable circumstances. Many treasure hunters make good finds 'after only five minutes searching' or 'walking back to the car' or 'having dreamt of treasure' and so on. I may have believed this to be exaggeration, if I hadn't started having similar experiences. Some put this phenomenon down to luck or coincidence, while others give it fancy names such as Serendipity, Assonance or the X-Factor. It happened so many times to me that I had to know more about the nature of this phenomenon and whether it could be harnessed? Then I heard about dowsing.

When I looked into dowsing it wasn't just about specially gifted people finding water, as I thought, almost anybody could find absolutely anything large or small. The best treasure dowsers could locate treasure, hundreds or even thousands of miles away using a simple tool with a map, then go out into the field and dig it up.

I read a few books on dowsing, most were obsessive about finding water, some were rather academic, there were one or two practical guides on the techniques of dowsing but almost nothing on treasure dowsing. I bought a pair of L-shaped rods and tried to follow the instructions with little effect. I didn't know what the problem was at the time and assumed I was one of the very few people unable to dowse. Looking back, the problem was the instructions or the instructor who had devised the most impractical way imaginable to use a pair of L-rods.

I all but forgot about dowsing until I heard about Jim Longton, who was offering to dowse maps for a small fee or percentage of the finds. As an experiment, I sent Jim a map of a field, which had already yielded some treasure. A while later Jim phoned me: "There's gold and silver everywhere." He said, excitedly. When the map arrived back, it was littered with crosses, some indicated iron but most indicated non-ferrous metal. Immediately, I noticed that most of the crosses were concentrated in the area where I had already made finds and a row of ferrous crosses coincided with a row of iron stakes on the site. Jim lived 300 miles away and had never visited the site, I hadn't told him anything about the site either, so how did he know? Using Jim's map I doubled the amount of finds I recovered from the site.

More importantly, as well as the map, Jim had sent me instructions on how to make and use L-rods for treasure dowsing. Jim's instructions clearly showed he knew what he was talking about. I followed his guidance and quickly learned to dowse. I confess to being a poor dowser compared to Jim. Even so my treasure hunting success rate has improved remarkably to the extent that I can now treasure hunt whenever I want.

Throughout this manual, I have drawn on my own and others' experience in the practical use of dowsing to aid the finding of treasure. You do not need to learn to dowse yourself, you can easily find a dowser to do the job or use this manual to teach a friend or relative. This is a practical guide to the best ideas for supercharging your treasure hunting; use them and I guarantee you will be amazed at the results. **Good Hunting!**

A BRIEF HISTORY OF DOWSING

Dowsing has been recorded since the time of Moses, for the story of Aaron producing water from the rock (Exodus chapter 17, verse 6) is often quoted as the first written evidence. Even if we dismiss the Biblical claim, dowsers appear engraved on ancient Egyptian stonework and on the statue of a Chinese emperor dating circa 2200BC. Little else of dowsing is recorded until Agricola, in 1556, wrote *De Re Metallica*, a book on mining, which included an illustration of a German dowser at work:

Almost a hundred years after Agricola, Martine de Bertereau, Baroness de Beausoleil travelled Europe, with her husband, locating mineral deposits by dowsing. They discovered over 150 ore deposits of iron, gold and silver in France alone, before being imprisoned for practising the 'black arts'. Later, in the same century, a particularly interesting book was written by Jean Nicholas de Grenoble published in Lyons in 1691 under the title of *La Verge de Jacob or L'arte de Trouver les Trésors: Les Sources, les Limites, les Métaux, les Mines, les Minéraux et autres choses cachés par L'usage du Baton fourché.* (The Rod of Jacob or the art of finding treasure, springs, boundaries, metals, mines, minerals and other hidden things, by the use of the forked twig). Dowsing then seems to have sunk back into obscurity, although, undoubtedly it continued to be practised, at least for finding of water – the lifeblood of all living things – practised in secrecy, perhaps, because of its occult associations and the Church's condemnation as the work of the devil.

Victorian scientific interest aided by a softening of the Church's attitude brought dowsing out into the open. In 1874, Thomas Welton translated and published Jean Nicholas' book in English. During the following decades a number of respected men, including the physicist, Albert Einstein, performed impressive feats with a variety of dowsing devices. Most of these feats were only of academic value but by the middle of the 20th century dowsing was regularly being put to a great variety of profitable uses.

Farmer J W Young convinced wild-catter, Ace Gutowski, that oil lay beneath West Edmond, Oklahoma by demonstration with a goatskin-covered bottle hung from a watch chain which invariably swung from north to south when over oil. As a result, in 1943, Gutowski drilled a hole and discovered the largest oil deposit in Oklahoma for 20 years. And that is just one of very many examples of oil strikes by dowsers.

Colonel Harry Grattan, CBE, Royal Engineers was given the task of building a new Headquarters for the British Rhine Army at Mönchen Gladbach, Germany in 1952. Planning for at least 9000 people who would need 750,000 gallons of water per day was a major project. Water supply was a big problem. Notwithstanding that the British Army preferred the security of it's own water supply, the three local waterworks would have had to upgrade their equipment and pass the costs on in the form of water rates at £20,000 a year. A considerable sum at that time.

Colonel Grattan knew of a nearby family with a private well, which produced better quality water than any of the waterworks. He employed a geologist with the intention of tapping this source but a trial bore produced very little water. The Colonel was a proficient dowser, however, and decided to use his skills to solve the problem. Using the traditional forked twig the colonel began dowsing and getting reactions everywhere to the west of the test bore. On the strength of this, two further trial bores were executed with spectacular results.

The trials showed that the ground was mainly solid clay, but between 73 and 96 feet down there was an aquifer, which produced a copious supply of excellent quality water. The German government, responsible for site construction, were less than convinced by such surveying techniques and were adamant that the water supply would soon dry up. Gaining the support of his superior, General Sugden, Colonel Grattan was able to continue his exploration. Dowsing from horseback, the colonel plotted out the full extent of the aquifer, which extended to within a few hundred yards of two of the waterworks. The British Rhine Army's private waterworks were constructed providing the Army with all the water it needed and savings running into millions of pounds over the years.

Somewhat closer to our quest for buried objects was the work of Major General Scott Elliot, a former president of the British Society of Dowsers who spent many years finding previously unknown archaeological sites by dowsing. His initial plan was that he would find the sites and then hand them over for professional excavation. On discovering that the professionals were not interested, partly through scepticism and partly because they had more than enough sites of their own, the major learned to do his own excavations. He also discovered he could save enormous amounts of time and effort by mapping out the site features by dowsing before he removed the first sod. Nothing spectacular in terms of finds of great intrinsic value were ever reported but nevertheless, over a period of some 20 years the major discovered and excavated an impressive list of sites.

The fairly recent development of treasure hunting as a popular hobby has drawn one or two dowsers to the challenge of using their skills to find buried metal artefacts. In the USA, Louis J Matacia is a surveyor who has studied dowsing for years. During the Vietnam War he was commissioned to teach dowsing skills to US Marines so that they could avoid booby traps, navigate safely through jungles and learn the whereabouts of the enemy. Soldiers reported that using the L-rod in this way saved many lives. Louis is particularly interested in the challenge of the search. Using his dowsing together with a range of scientific devices he has located lost pipes, oil, wells, caves and buried treasures.

The most successful treasure dowser in Britain is Jim Longton from Lancashire. Jim took up dowsing when he retired from the wrestling ring and first hit the headlines in 1990 after finding a spectacular hoard of Viking silver brooches valued at over £40,000 ($80,000). His latest find is potentially Britain's Tutankhamen: a seventeenth century shipwreck, believed to contain untold treasures, including a 230 piece gilt-silver dinner service once owned by Charles I. While divers work on the recovery, Jim is being kept busy locating more treasure wrecks for a marine salvage company. I am certain we will soon be hearing of Jim making more magnificent dowsing finds.

JIM LONGTON IN ACTION

HOW DOES DOWSING WORK?

No one knows how dowsing works, they only know it does. Mankind does not know everything. Much science fact today was the science fiction and mysticism of the past and dowsing has undoubtedly survived from primitive times when the ability to find water, for instance, could have meant the difference between life and death.

There are two popular theories to explain dowsing: the first suggests that dowsing works as a result of natural phenomena. Buried metal, minerals and underground water cause either a magnetic field or a disturbance in the Earth's own magnetic field. The dowsing rod is just an amplifying tool for the reaction of the natural magnetic field in the body to the magnetic field in the ground.

This theory was investigated scientifically in Logan, Utah, USA, around 30 years ago. Intrigued by a dowser pinpointing the bodies of two boys who drowned in a local river, Duane G. Chadwick, professor at the Utah State University Water Research Laboratory undertook several experiments to try and determine the science behind dowsing. Chadwick and his colleague, Larry Jensen started from the fact that geologists had discovered that water below the ground can disrupt the Earth's natural magnetic field. They figured that dowsers could show sensitivity to these disruptions by involuntary muscular movement in the wrists and dowsing rods would certainly amplify any small muscular reaction by as much as 300 times.

In the first of a series of experiments, on the Campus, Chadwick and Jensen tested their idea that dowsing reactions might occur at places where the Earth's magnetic field changed. They prepared a straight track, free of obstructions and, using caesium vapour magnetometer checks at one-foot intervals, ensured that the Earth's magnetic field was stable for the entire length of the course. Chadwick then buried a length of wire, in a neutral area, to distort the magnetic field. Twenty-five participants, picked at random from the university students and staff, hardly any of them known dowsers, were put to the test using wire clothes-hangers modified into a pair of L-shaped rods held out more or less horizontally. They were told that if the rods moved, they must stop and place a small wooden block at their feet. The results were amazing in that 23 of the participants had a dowsing reaction within three feet of the buried wire. As Chadwick remarked: "With odds like that you could break the bank."

In a further experiment Chadwick and Jensen marked out a test course with no obvious or known features. This time, the test was double blind – in that nothing was deliberately buried and no one knew what was out there. 150 people, recruited as before from the university students and staff and given dowsing rods, were asked to drop a wooden block whenever they experienced a dowsing reaction and again almost everyone did. On average they dropped 11.3 blocks each and the location of each block was documented. Then Chadwick and Jensen went over the course with two magnetometers mounted, at different heights, on a wooden sled. The difference between the magnetometer readings showed the variation in the magnetic field along the track walked by the dowsers. The researchers then graphed the magnetometer readings against the positions of the wooden blocks, which showed again that the dowsing reactions occurred unmistakably at peaks in the magnetic field.

The Second theory is that dowsing works through the arts of the paranormal; an explanation used to account for the ability of some dowsers to find objects which are thought not to produce or influence magnetic fields. As far as field dowsing (i.e. dowsing in close proximity to the object or substance being sought) is concerned, the paranormal theory is probably in error since it has been shown that virtually everything, be it animal, vegetable or mineral, reacts to magnetic fields.

Map dowsing is probably the most difficult phenomenon to explain. How does a person dowse a map and successfully locate a target hundreds or even thousands of miles away? There are many unanswered questions along the same lines, which are commonly put down to psychic ability or intuition. Map dowsing could, however, be explained using the magnetic effect theory. Radio waves, which are, after all, a form of electromagnetic radiation, travel over great distances, unseen and unheard; so why not dowsing waves?

There could actually be two types of dowsing: field dowsing based on magnetic effects and map dowsing or distance dowsing based on intuition or psychic ability. The two types of dowsing are quite different and both types can be learned and improve with perseverance and practice.

I suppose it would be nice to know how dowsing actually works but does it really matter? Do all drivers know how an internal combustion engine works and would that knowledge make any difference to their driving skills? The same argument applies to dowsing – you only have to use the technology to produce spectacular results.

I'll end with a quote from the renowned physicist, Albert Einstein:

> I know very well that many scientists consider dowsing as they do astrology, as a type of ancient superstition. According to my conviction this is, however unjustified. The dowsing rod is a simple instrument which shows the reaction of the human nervous system to certain factors which are unknown at this time.

FINDING AND USING A DOWSER

The object of this manual is really to show you how to dowse and then to use dowsing to help find *treasure*, whatever the word *treasure* may mean to you. Having said that, you may want the results without doing your own dowsing. Instead of or as well as learning to dowse, alternatives might be to find someone amongst your family or friends who would have a go or consult an amateur or professional dowser. I must admit that I chose the latter before I did any dowsing to speak of, as I wanted to see just what a dowser could achieve.

The advantage of using an accomplished dowser is that it is likely to be the most successful in the short term. There are disadvantages however:

- You will have to pay a modest fee or a percentage of your resulting finds.
- You may have to wait until the dowser can fit you in.
- If you don't ask the right questions to start with, you may not get useful information back.

Dowsers tend to specialise; most are interested in finding water. If water is your treasure, fine, find a water dowser. If you prefer your treasure more metallic then you need a dowser interested in finding metal. You wouldn't call a plumber to fix your television, after all. Occasionally dowsers advertise in the treasure hunting press and these dowsers are worth looking out for, because they probably have the right skills and interests. A quicker way of finding a suitable dowser is to contact your national dowsing society. These societies are always very approachable and helpful since they exist mainly to promote dowsing and find work for their members. You will, of course, need to specify, in broad terms, what you want the dowser to do. For instance, what do you want the dowser to look for and do you want him to dowse a map or look for something out in the field. It's always worth trying to find a dowser near at hand even if you are only interested in having a map dowsed. You'll see later on that inaccuracies creep into map dowsing, which may only be overcome by dowsing on site. I can assure you that there is little so frustrating as being told where something desirable is buried and not being able to find it.

When you have found your dowser you will need to come to some arrangement to recompense them for their time and expenses. Some ask for a fee, others a percentage of the resulting recovery, it's up to you to negotiate, however I have always found that dowsers love to dowse and as a result they don't expect excessively high rewards. If you find a proficient dowser, you will get exceptional value for money and probably a good friend.

THE PENDULUM

A pendulum can, in the hands of a good map dowser, pinpoint the position of anything buried; from a single coin to a lost city, many miles away. For the treasure hunter, this aspect of dowsing holds enormous potential for locating sites, regardless of their state of cultivation and without the need of permission. Further, once any necessary permission has been obtained, the same technique can be used to plot the treasure content of the site, facilitating rapid retrieval.

All you need to start is a pendulum, which is basically a weight on a line that acts as a little computer, moving in different ways according to the information you require:

- It will move in a circle in response to a buried or hidden object either over a map or out in the field.
- It may differentiate between objects; ferrous and non-ferrous for example, by gyrating clockwise for one type or anti clockwise for another.
- It will respond similarly to unambiguous questions phrased so that the answer ought to be only yes or no.
- It can indicate a direction by oscillation.

You can use many things found around the home to make a pendulum. Pendants, rings, fishing weights, hexagonal nuts, cotton reels, buttons all make perfectly acceptable pendulums.

HEXAGONAL NUT, WOODEN CAVITY AND QUARTZ PENDULUMS

There are a few points to consider, however:

- The nearer the shape of the weight is to a builder's plumb bob, the better it will perform mechanically.
- Natural materials, such as wood or crystal for the weight and cotton or silk for the line, are claimed to be preferable to artificial materials. Having said that; many pendulums are made from brass – a man-made alloy!
- All things being equal, a favourite personal object or one of sentimental value will make a good pendulum. Professional dowser Jim Longton, uses a cross he normally wears around his neck.
- You could use an object made from the same metal that you are seeking.

- Some dowsers prefer to use a cavity pendulum, which has a chamber to hold a sample of what you are seeking; a silver or gold coin can be dropped in, for instance.

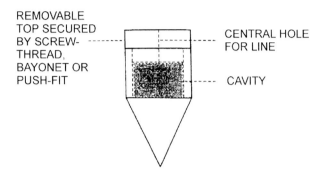

REMOVABLE TOP SECURED BY SCREW-THREAD, BAYONET OR PUSH-FIT

CENTRAL HOLE FOR LINE

CAVITY

Cavity pendulum turned from hardwood, e.g. Beech. Dimensions are 2.5 x 1.25 inches (6.5cm x 3.25cm). NB. Avoid using metal in its construction or you may find only nails!

- The larger the pendulum, the larger the circle it will describe. This is of little consequence for most uses but a large pendulum will be less accurate than a small one for pinpointing when used directly over a map.
- You can purchase ready-made pendulums from New Age shops or Dowsing Societies.
- You could ask a wood turner or a jeweller to make you one.

If you have any trouble deciding, just pick an object close to plumb-bob shape; once you have learned how to use the pendulum you can experiment with different objects and materials. When you have chosen your weight, assuming it is not already suspended, you need to fix a line to it. Cotton, wool, silk or sisal string will all do fine. The usual operating length of a pendulum line is about four inches (10cm), however, it is advisable to make the line around 10 inches (25cm) long to allow adjustment to find the best operating length for yourself. You can trim it down later if you wish but meanwhile just keep the excess out of the way of the moving weight. Bear in mind that longer lines allow the pendulum to describe larger circles and beware the advice of those who claim that success in locating gold, for instance, is dependent on the line length. A popular myth is that the line length required for finding gold is 44 inches (112cm). Try it by all means but you will probably find it unworkable as the pendulum tends to wrap itself around your leg and you are too far away to clearly see the map you are trying to dowse.

The most popular way to hold the pendulum is to pinch the line, between your thumb and forefinger, as if the line is a pinch of salt to be sprinkled on food. Keep your thumb and forefinger still though, don't sprinkle. Another way of holding the pendulum is to hold your hand as a pretend pistol. Extend your forefinger and run the line over the top and down the back of your forefinger clamping with your thumb, about an inch from the end of your finger. The way you hold the pendulum is unimportant providing the weight is free to move on the end of it's line. The best way to hold the pendulum is the way that feels most comfortable to you.

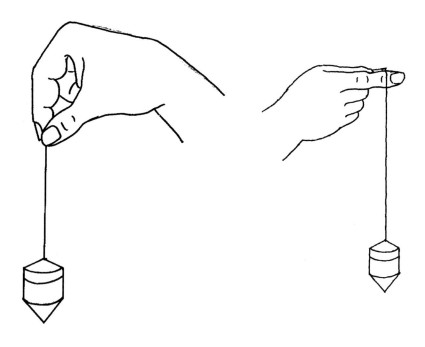

Pendulum responses vary from person to person. You will need to establish what your pendulum's responses mean to you by asking it some questions. Before we get to that I should say something about the strange idea of holding conversations with normally inanimate objects such as dowsing devices. The given advice is to talk to them as a pet, normally kindly but scold if necessary. To anyone who ever owned a pet rock this should present no problem. If you find talking out loud to your dowsing devices embarrassing, then just think your questions, it makes no difference. We come back to the point that I cannot emphasise enough – you must be comfortable with what you are doing. As the pendulum can't react instantly to a stimulus, it improves the response time if you apply a little force to keep the pendulum oscillating gently backwards and forwards in a rocking motion, towards you and away from you. This is called 'idling'.

With your pendulum idling, ask it to show you yes, no & don't know. Typically, the pendulum will circle clockwise for yes, anti-clockwise for no and oscillate in a straight line for don't know. If the pendulum won't respond or gives the same response regardless of what you ask, you will need to train it. Take a piece of blank paper and draw a circle about two inches (5cm) diameter then hold the pendulum above the circle and persuade the pendulum to follow the circle in both clockwise and anticlockwise directions. Cheat, if you must and physically force the pendulum to circle.

Draw a large cross (+) on the paper, mark the points North, South, East, West and orientate the paper as near as possible to the true compass points. Ask the pendulum to show you the points, one by one. If you get an identical response on opposite points, for example, North – South you can ask the pendulum to differentiate by saying something like "Is that North?" The pendulum's yes response would confirm North; the no response – South.

Here are a couple of exercises worth doing to help train yourself to use the pendulum:

Line up three, or more, upturned opaque cups and find someone to hide a coin beneath one of them, while you are out of the room. Hold your pendulum over each one in turn and ask: "Is there a coin beneath this cup?" When you frequently obtain a yes response over the cup with the coin under it, you are starting to get somewhere.

Here's one you can do on your own. Take a pack of playing cards, shuffle them and place them face down on a table in front of you. Hold the pendulum over the top card and ask "Is the top card a red card?" If the response is yes, remove the top card and place it on the table, face down, at the right of the pack; if the response is no, place the card on the left. Repeat the exercise until you have gone through the entire pack. If you look at the right hand pile of cards they should be predominantly hearts and diamonds. Count the number of red cards and the total number of cards in the right hand pile. Your percentage success rate can be calculated by dividing the number of red cards by the total number of cards in the right hand pile and multiplying by 100. Eg. 16 reds in a total of 26 would be 62%, which is about my current success rate; not brilliant but a useful 12% better than random selection.

Just a few comments on a couple of points I mentioned at the beginning of this chapter:

- You can train the pendulum to automatically distinguish between ferrous and non-ferrous metals when dowsing directly over a map if you find that useful but remember treasure was sometimes buried in iron containers. However, to do this you just have to ask the pendulum to show you ferrous metal and non-ferrous metal in turn, to determine which way your pendulum gyrates for the type of metal.

- The pendulum can be used to guide you to treasure out in the field by the direction of its oscillation. By that I mean the pendulum will oscillate in a direct line between you and the treasure you are seeking so you can just follow the direction of swing until you reach the treasure, when the pendulum will let you know by changing from oscillation into gyration. I don't personally find this so easy as using an L-rod which we will be covering next, however a pendulum can be much more easily and discreetly carried than an L-rod. Don't leave home without one!

THE L-ROD

While, as a generalisation, all dowsing tools can be used for all types of dowsing, the pendulum is best used for map dowsing and the L-rod for field dowsing. The basic L-rod is simply a length of stiff metal wire or thin round bar bent into the shape of the letter 'L', hence the name, although some might argue that it is an abbreviation of Locator Rod. Traditionally the short arm of the 'L' is held in a loose fist while the long arm projects forward over the top of the fist. There are a few variations on the basic design and my personal preference is one that Jim Longton uses and has kindly allowed me to reproduce here. If you already have a pair of L-rods you are happy with, by all means use them or you can make excellent rods as follows:

You will need 22" (56cm) of round metal bar (brass is considered best) of diameter 1/16" (1.5mm) to 3/16" (5mm) to make each rod. Unless you have easy access to round bar, I suggest you use two wire clothes hangers. (NB Measurements and angles do not need to be too precise to make a working rod):

- Invert the first hanger and measure 14" (36cm) from one side, along the horizontal bar then mark and cut through with a pair of pliers or a junior hacksaw. Measure 22" (56cm) back from the first cut and make a second cut. Discard the hooked portion. Smooth the cut ends with a file or emery cloth. (Fig 1)

Fig 1

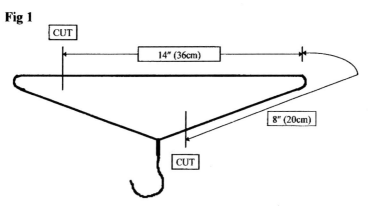

- Using a pair of pliers or a vice, first straighten and then bend the shorter arm back to an angle of 135°. (Fig 2)

Fig 2

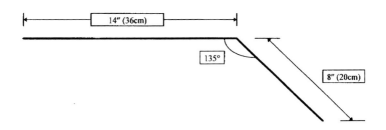

- From the cut end, measure 7" (18cm) along the shorter arm, and bend this portion back until horizontal. (Fig 3)

Fig 3

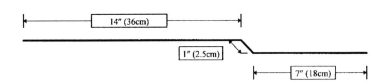

- Turn the last 5.5" (14cm) up at right angles. Finally, turn the last 0.5" (1cm) of the upright inwards, at right angles. (Fig 4)

Fig 4

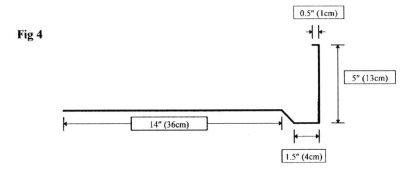

- Lay the rod on a level surface and adjust it until it lies reasonably flat.
- Make a second rod from the other coat hanger.

Health warning: The rods are perfectly harmless when used as described. If you wish to use them to play Conan the Barbarian, Robin Hood, Ivanhoe or act out any other fantasy, don't blame me if you puncture your eyeball or any other part of your body. I would suggest that children using the rods should be supervised by a responsible adult. The rods can be made extra safe by folding their tips downwards or back on themselves, wrapping their tips with insulating tape or applying a blob of a resin such as Araldite™.

HOLDING THE RODS

Take the short arm of a rod in each hand so that the long arm is on the opposite side to your thumbs. Clench your fists around them loosely and turn your wrists so that your thumbs are uppermost and the long arm projects forward from the bottom of your fist. Tuck your elbows into your body and keep your upper arms in line with your body. Hold your forearms straight out in front of you, the width of your body apart and at whatever angle necessary to keep the rods reasonably parallel to the ground. The rods should now be pointing forward like extensions of your forearms. You may need to adjust your grip so that the rods are just free to move but not sloppy.

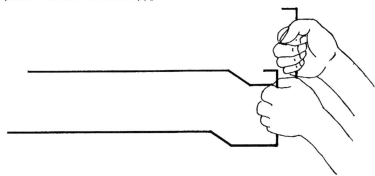

When you are happy with holding the rods we can move on to some dowsing exercises:

- Hold the rods in the normal dowsing position as just described. Ask the rods to turn left. After they have moved, restart the rods pointing forward. The easy way to get the rods to point forward is to drop your forearms so that the rods point to the ground then raise your forearms back to the horizontal. Ask the rods to turn right. Restart. Ask the rods to cross. The rods will cross on your chest. Practise until the rods move easily.
- Place a coin on the floor then take a few paces back from it. Hold your rods in the normal dowsing position and walk slowly toward the coin saying: 'I am looking for a coin'. The rods will either cross as you pass immediately over the coin or within a few paces past the coin. Keep practising until the rods cross at the coin.
- Place a copper coin; a silver coin and a brass coin some distance apart on the ground. Hold your rods in the normal dowsing position and walk slowly toward the coin saying: 'I am looking for a copper coin'. The rods will cross as you pass over the copper coin but not the other two. Repeat the exercise with the silver coin and then the brass coin. Keep practising until you can differentiate between various metals.
- Stand sideways to a distant building or other large object that you know the location of and ask the rods to show you where it is. Give the full name of the place, i.e. 'Show me St. James' Church'. Clear your mind of everything else and concentrate. Once you get this to work, try standing with your back to the 'target' (as dowsers tend to call objects they are trying to find) and see what happens.
- When you have succeeded with the previous exercise, take your rods to the gate of a field or any other open space where you have any necessary search permission. Hold the rods as normal and ask: 'are there any coins buried in this field?' Normally the rods will cross for *yes* and move apart or open out for *no*. As with the pendulum you

may need to determine what the rods' movement, or lack of it, means for you. Ask the rods to point to the nearest coin, then walk slowly in the direction indicated by the rods, turning, as necessary, to keep the rods pointing straight out in front of you. On reaching the coin the rods will cross. If you want to search for other objects as well as coins, ask the rods to find *treasure*.

Keep practising. Once you can obtain a response from the rods in all these exercises, you are basically ready to do anything. Even if you can't do it all at first, you should find that the rods will produce some useful results in the field and you will improve with time.

You may have noticed that in the last exercise, you located your first buried treasure but how do you recover it? It is almost essential to use a metal detector for final location of metallic objects, as pinpointing by dowsing alone is rarely precise. If you are looking for non-metallic treasures than that is a different ball game and unless you can devise your own pinpointing technique, presumably you are just going to have to dig for it. The drawback of using two rods is that you have no hands free to carry anything so, hopefully you will have brought someone else along, who can, at least, carry a metal detector and extraction tool, and perhaps do the digging for you. If you are the independent sort, you don't need to have a partner, it's very easy to both dowse and recover targets by yourself using a metal detector and one of the following methods:

- Dowse and mark first, detect and dig second. You will need a couple of dozen two-foot long pea sticks from a garden centre and something in which to carry them on your back or hip. I use an archery quiver but I am sure most of you could make or adapt something for carrying the sticks if you wanted to save about £20. All you do then is dowse and mark where the rods cross by pushing a stick into the ground. When you run out of sticks, set your detector up and detect from stick to stick, collecting the sticks as you go, as well as the finds.

- You can dowse with just one rod, believe it or not. The great advantage with single rod dowsing is that you have one hand free to use a metal detector, so you can both dowse and detect simultaneously. All you have to do is to sweep with the detector using one hand while holding the rod in your other hand. To recover what you detect you only have to find a means of carrying a digging tool, without using your hands. A tool-belt works fine.

While we are on the subject of recovery, I ought to mention some of the pitfalls. A metal detector will not be able to detect every target that you dowse. Dowsing goes far deeper than metal detectors. I have heard of match head sized silver objects, dowsed at depths of three feet and I have dowsed targets that only produced a signal from a detector after I had dug out a foot depth of soil first. You can, of course, just dig a hole wherever your rods indicate a target but, unless you are looking for something specific like a suspected hoard, you are likely to find this approach counter productive as it could take a couple of hours to dig each hole. I fit the largest suitable search-head to my detector; if a search for a target doesn't produce a signal, I just leave it and go on to the next target. I couldn't have made the find anyway, had I only used a detector.

Recently disturbed ground can be quite frustrating to dowse owing to a phenomenon called remanence. When an object is removed from the ground, dowsing rods still react to the spot where it lay for about a fortnight, in my experience. Conversely, when an object is placed in the ground it takes a similar amount of time before rods will react to it. Beware freshly ploughed fields, detecting rallies and the dry sands of beaches in summer!

So far as search techniques are concerned there are several approaches depending on the type of site and your temperament.

- Theoretically you should be able to just follow the rods or rod from one good target to the next, by moving your body to keep your forearm(s) in line with the rod(s). This is probably the easiest way and it is excellent for checking out a site for the first time. However, unless you are really good at discriminating you will miss a lot of desirable targets.

- There is a more systematic approach for dowsing with two rods and one that is almost essential for searching sites like orchards or woodland, where you are unable to walk around unrestricted. Search in straight lines about two metres or two yards apart; the rods will cross if you walk over a target or there is a target to the left or right of you. Just put a stick in the ground at your feet as a marker whenever the rods cross. When you come to look for the target you need to detect a circle around your marker at least twice the width between your search lines. Your detecting area should be four metres diameter if your search lines are two metres apart. If you are searching an orchard, for example, there is no need to fight your way through the trees trying to detect for targets which you suspect lie in the next row. You can deal with such targets when you come to search that row. If you are searching open land it will help to define your detecting areas if you leave your markers in place until you have finished recovering targets. You should then end up having lines of markers to follow in place of the natural lines, formed by the trees in an orchard (FIG. 1).

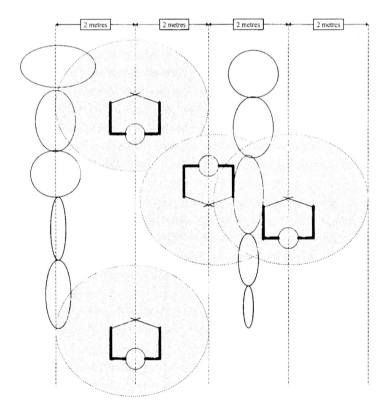

FIG 1: SYSTEMATIC DOWSING WITH TWO RODS. DETECT SHADED AREAS.

- You can improve on this two-rod method a little by making the initial target location a two-stage process. Every time your rods cross, restart the rods and ask them to point at the target. Then, when you push your marker stick into the ground, lean it in the direction indicated by the rods. That will halve the search area as you only need to detect on the left side or the right side of the marker, depending on which way it is leaning.

- I find systematic dowsing with a single rod easier than using two rods since the single rod actually points at the target to tell you there is something there. Also a single rod is less sensitive than two, which helps reduce the amount of less desirable targets and automatically you are given a more precise target location. For orchards and the like, search in straight lines as with two rods; as you approach a target the rod will start to turn. Walk slowly on until the rod is just pointing behind you, by which time you will probably have lost control of it and it will be resting against your arm. Put a marker in at your feet, leaning it to the left if the rod turned left or to the right if the rod turned right. Walk forward a couple of paces so that you are well clear of the target, then turn yourself around 180 degrees so that you are facing the way you have just come. Restart the rod and retrace your steps slowly past your marker until the rod turns to point behind you once again. Place another marker leaning to the side the rod pointed. You should now have two markers, leaning in the same direction which, theoretically, form the two ends of the base line of a triangle with the target lying at the apex. There is no need to worry about the trigonometry. When you return with your metal detector, just search all the area between the two markers and from the markers out to the tree line. (FIG. 2)

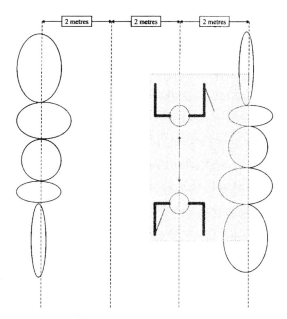

FIG 2:DOWSING WITH A SINGLE ROD. DETECT SHADED AREA.

- For searching open land with a single rod you can use the "boxing-in" method. If you also carry a metal detector you only need half a dozen small marker sticks that you could carry in your finds pouch. Search in lines two metres apart as before. When the rod starts to turn, keep walking until the rod is pointing behind you (as previously). Put down a marker, turn yourself 90 degrees in the direction that the rod pointed, back off a couple of paces so that the rod isn't influenced immediately by the target, restart the rod and walk slowly on until it turns again to the same side as previously. Put down another marker. Repeat the process twice more and you should then have four markers in the ground with each marker forming a corner of a rectangle or box. Theoretically the target will lie at the centre of the box but detect the entire area of the box in case there is more than one target. (FIG. 3).

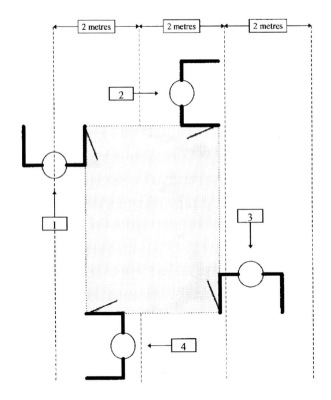

FIG 3: THE BOXING-IN METHOD. DETECT SHADED AREA

In the last two methods, you will quite often find that after you've placed a marker, your rod unexpectedly swings to the "wrong" side. This is caused by there being two or more targets in close proximity. When this happens, place a marker; restart the rod and continue walking until the rod swings to the "correct" side then place another marker. When you have finished marking the first target, you can go back to the "out of place" marker and dowse for the second target. All you have to do now is recover your treasures.

Before we leave the L-rod I'd like to say something about possible improvements. In addition to changing the basic rod design from the traditional up-and-over to the 'under-slung', there are three basic areas that might be altered to bring enhanced performance: adjust the length, change the pivot and use a sample of what you seek:

- Optimum length of the horizontal section of the rod is probably determined more by who the user is than what is being looked for. Range is another possible consideration in that longer rods will locate (i.e. indicate a target) from a greater distance than shorter. The easy way to determine the optimum length for you is to ask the rods: 'Are these rods the right length for me (or for seeking *treasure*)?' Depending on the response you may have to question further: 'Should they be shorter? Longer? One inch shorter? Etc..' Then just make the rods the correct length. If you need a variable length rod, I have seen commercial rods consisting of a handle with a selection of screw on rods of different length and I don't believe it is beyond the wit of man to make rods from simple telescopic car aerials.

- You can make the rods move easier and as a result more sensitive by fitting sleeves to the handles (the upright portion). *Bic* type biro cases are good for this purpose if you chop off the tapered end. You can just slip the sleeves on to conventional rods but on the 'Longton' design, discussed earlier, you will have to unbend and remake the top stop or make the complete rod anew in order to fit the sleeves. You will see later, however, that increasing sensitivity may not be such a good idea. Ask the rods if they would be better for you if they moved more easily.

FIG 4

Plastic Sleeve

Sample Chamber

The instructions for one pair of commercial rods I bought told me that if I wanted to find coins, I should put a coin in a plastic bag and hang it on the end of one of the rods. This ill-conceived instruction would probably give a beginner a hard time. Dowsing tools are mechanical devices and you give yourself the best chance of using them successfully if you aid the mechanical operation rather than hinder it. Also consider the comfort factor and resist the temptation to hold a sample in your hand while trying to dowse. If you like the idea of using a sample the best way is to fit, or have fitted, a small sample pot at the handle end of the rod. (FIG 4) You must use the same metal that the rods are made from or you will have a thermocouple generating electricity, again interfering with your dowsing. For a sample chamber, you might try taping a plastic film canister to the rod near to the handle.

As you practice dowsing you may find that the tools become too sensitive for you and you may need to make them less sensitive to suit your enhanced skills. Shortening rods and pendulum strings usually reduces sensitivity but you can only go so far else the device won't work mechanically. Ultimately you may be able to dowse without using any devices at all. Although it was fiction, the television soap series *Dallas* featured an oil dowser named 'Digger' Barnes who used nothing but his hands to find the oil which made the Ewings rich. I have personally experienced a tingling sensation in my hand when passing it over a target on a map and there are several real-life dowsers who use only their hands to make finds.

MAP DOWSING

The first thing you need to do when map dowsing is to decide what you want to find. Are you looking for sites, a hoard or individual coins and artefacts? You will need to select or scale your map accordingly to the size of your target. You wouldn't expect to pinpoint a single coin on a map of an entire county any more than locate a deserted medieval village on a plan of your back garden. For dowsing hoards or individual artefacts you need to use a 1:1267 (50" to one mile) scale or larger. For dowsing sites, 1:10560 (6" to one mile) is ideal. If you haven't a map of the right scale, you can adjust it easily by either enlarging or reducing using a photocopier or a pantograph drawing device. Aim to have the final map around A4 size (297mm x 210mm or 12" x 8").

As usual, there is more than one way to dowse a map and you can use a pendulum or single L-rod. The traditional way, using a pendulum, is to comfortably position yourself over the map, sitting, kneeling or standing. With the pendulum idling, very slowly move it over the map systematically, while concentrating on what you wish to find. Every time the pendulum gyrates, you mark a cross on the map as near as you can to the centre of the circle that the pendulum is describing. You will find it helpful, for eventual recovery, if you mark on the map the direction of pendulum travel, since pinpointing is usually way-off target in that direction. The reason for this is that it takes time for the pendulum to start gyrating in order to indicate a target; meanwhile the pendulum is still moving forward. If you take four minutes to cover one mile on the map, relatively speaking, the pendulum is travelling at 15 mph. Imagine running a four-minute mile across a field, while trying to spot a coin dropped somewhere on the surface. Even if you manage to see the coin, by the time you have realised and stopped, the coin will be some way behind you.

The map dowsing method I prefer uses a fine grid to divide the map into manageable sectors of rows and columns. An easy way to put a suitable grid onto the map is to photocopy a quadrille ruled (1/4" or 5mm squares) sheet of paper onto an A4 copy of the map. Better still, you will get the grid on the map in one pass, if you photocopy the quadrille ruling onto a clear acetate sheet, then photocopy your maps through the acetate. If you haven't got access to a photocopier and don't want to pay the library or print shop for photocopying, you can simply draw a grid on your map with a pencil and ruler.

To dowse the map simply point with a pencil or pen at one end of each row in turn and with either the pendulum or L-rod in your other hand, ask: 'Is there any treasure in this row?' I use the word treasure, for an unspecified desirable metal object. Feel free to ask for whatever you want to find by any name you choose, as long as it means something to you. Every time you get a yes response from your dowsing tool, place a tick at the end of the appropriate row. When you have checked all the rows, repeat the exercise with each column. If there is only one treasure on your map it will be located at the intersection of your ticked row and your ticked column. You will probably have more than one treasure on your map, which will involve a little more questioning of your dowsing tool. If you have three ticked rows and three ticked columns, then you have nine possible treasure locations, each at the intersection of every ticked row with every ticked column. To sort the real from the possible, you point to each intersection in turn and ask: 'Is there treasure buried here?' Mark all your yes responses and there you have it.

	✓		✓			✓	
✓	NO		X			NO	
✓	X		NO			NO	
✓	NO		NO			X	

There is another map dowsing method particularly useful in looking for a single treasure. This is more suitable for the L-rod although the pendulum can be used with slightly less accuracy. You need a ruler for this one, a rolling ruler preferably and a writing implement. All you do is to slowly move the ruler across the map asking your L-rod or pendulum to indicate when the leading edge of the ruler meets the treasure you seek. When the rod swings or the pendulum gyrates you stop moving the ruler and draw a line on the map along the leading edge of the ruler. Turn the ruler through 90° so that it is across the line you have just drawn and, starting at one end of the line run the ruler slowly along it while asking for the treasure on the leading edge. Again, when your L-rod or pendulum indicates, stop moving the ruler and draw another line down the ruler's leading edge. Your treasure is located at the intersection of the two lines.

Whichever way you dowse the map, if you want more information about the targets you have dowsed such as what metal it is, how deep or how old you only have to ask your pendulum or L-rod. Remember though that whichever tool you use it can only answer yes or no, so you need to phrase your questions carefully. For determining the metal you would just ask in turn: 'Is this treasure made of gold?' 'Is it made of silver?' Etc. For depth you would ask questions like: 'Is it more than three feet deep?' 'Is it less than two feet deep?' Then, assuming you had a no to both: 'Is it 24 inches deep?' Is it 25 inches deep?' And so on until you hit a yes.

All you have to do now is to find your targets and dig them. I don't know why it happens but even if you use accurate surveying equipment to translate the cross on your map onto mother earth, there is a good chance that the target won't be there! For example, on a 6 inch Ordnance Survey map Jim Longton dowsed for me, he identified six targets, which I have probably found. However, the distance between the targets on the map and the actual targets varied between zero and 220 metres.

Recently another dowser friend, Frank Delamere dowsed photographs of a treasure site with excellent results in that investigating Frank's predicted locations on the photographs I recovered a greater number of gold coins than had been found previously. Using a photograph instead of a map (Frank was 100 metres out when he dowsed a map of the site) seems infinitely more accurate and well worth the extra effort of taking the photograph.

Unless you just want to trust to luck that by searching in the right general area you may stumble across the target, the best way to successful recovery is to use dowsing rods. The best dowsers can stand at the field gate and ask the rods to show them where a particular target is buried, walk over to it and dig it up. The rest of us have to work a bit harder. Nevertheless, if you use your rods as described in the previous chapter, in the places dowsed on your maps or photographs, you may soon be recovering more treasure than you thought possible.

PHOTOGRAPHING TREASURE AURAS

If you ever wondered how South American civilisations, like the Incas, found all their gold and silver, the answer is that at the height of the full moon, the Indians would see a bluish-green flame glowing above the ground where precious metal was buried. The Indians and later the Spanish Conquistadors used these auras to locate large quantities of silver and gold. If you are not too keen on wandering about in the middle of the night hoping to chance upon an aura, there is an alternative – the Polaroid SX-70 camera.

The Polaroid SX-70 camera, by accident rather than design, has the ability to 'see' auras emanating from buried precious metals. The quantity of buried metal doesn't have to be large for I have photographed auras emanating form single gold coins. The only criterion is that the metal needs to have been buried for at least a couple of years. The SX-70 film, known as Time Zero Film in the USA; SX-70 Instant Film in Europe, is made to a different specification from other Polaroid films and the camera itself is, uniquely amongst Polaroid field cameras, a Single Lens Reflex (which means you look directly through the lens instead of a viewfinder). 'The only camera Polaroid ever made that was worth a damn!' Some say.

Unfortunately, the SX-70, a success of the 1970's is no longer in production and has to be sought out on the second-hand market. I bought mine for £30 ($60) through a wanted advertisement in my local 'freeads' paper and I spotted two others recently: one on Ebay, the Internet auction, with a starting price of £60 ($120) and a special edition SX-70, in the collectors section of a camera shop, priced at £89 ($175). Other places you might look for a camera to buy are: boot fairs, antique shops, flea markets, second-hand shops, charity shops and photographic equipment fairs. SX-70 film is still widely available at most camera shops, costing around £12 ($24) for a cartridge of ten exposures.

You will also need to get a UV filter to fit over the lens. There isn't a fitting on the lens to take a filter and as far as I know no filters were ever made for this camera, although there are clip on lenses which, if you get hold of one, could be adapted to take a filter. You won't go too far wrong if you take your camera to a camera shop and ask them to supply a filter a little larger in diameter than the lens; 30mm diameter is about right but check that the filter will fit your camera before you leave the shop. When you come to use the camera attach the filter with a couple of blobs of a solid reusable adhesive like 'Blu-Tack', one either side of the lens but not obscuring it. Don't stick the filter on with superglue or you won't be able to close the camera up. Finally, one accessory that it would be useful to have is a compass, it doesn't need to be fancy as you only have to identify North and South with it.

Having equipped yourself with SX-70 camera, film, UV filter and compass you only need a site where you think there could be gold or silver, which has been buried more than two years (the time it takes to generate an aura). The optimum condition for taking pictures is either early morning sunlight or late evening sunlight; foggy mornings are also said to produce good results. Presumably a low angle, of sunlight and possibly reduced light is needed for the camera to capture the aura. You may be successful outside of these conditions but if you don't know for sure where the treasure is you will give yourself the best chance if you follow the guidelines. You can always experiment later, when you have more experience.

Aim to be at your treasure site either at sunrise or a half-hour before sunset. Stand as close as you can to the area where you think precious metal may be buried and, using the compass, position yourself to the North or South of the target area so that you are at right angles to the sun. Focus the camera on the target area and take a photograph. As I am sure you know, Polaroid photographs are self processing and you will have your picture within a couple of minutes of clicking the shutter. Take a look at the photograph to see if it shows an aura. You may be lucky and get an aura first time or you may have to keep trying, perhaps shifting your position backwards or forwards or to the opposite side of the target area. Take a series of photographs over the half-hour period after sunrise or before sunset, if you need to. Persevere and you will soon find your aura and the treasure that produced it.

AURA FROM THE COVER OF LOUIS J MATACIA'S BOOK

The Polaroid SX-70 photographs below were taken on sites believed to hold gold treasures. The auras were gold or yellow in colour. On a site believed to hold a cache of silver coins, not yet recovered, auras on the photographs were purple in colour. If the camera produces an aura, regardless of the colour, I would suggest you try and uncover the source.

AURAS FROM A FIELD WHICH PRODUCED A SCATTER OF GOLD COINS

AURA FROM A POSSIBLE TREASURE WRECK SITE

TREASURE ENGINEERING

For a long time there has been a vague notion that seemingly insignificant events can lead to major occurrences further down the line. And matter or events quite often come together in groups against the statistical odds – your portion of fruit cake, for instance, may contain more cherries than all other identically sized portions from the same mix. Most would put these happenings down to coincidence although folklore has acknowledged the existence of the phenomenon from sayings about bad luck and buses coming in threes as well as the proverb:

> "For want of a nail, the shoe was lost;
> For want of a shoe, the horse was lost;
> For want of a horse, the rider was lost;
> For want of a rider the battle was lost;
> For want of a battle, the kingdom was lost!"

With the advent of computer technology, capable of performing millions of mundane calculations in short order, scientists have started investigating such pattern formations in apparently random systems calling it Chaos theory. An example called the 'butterfly effect' describes the scenario that a butterfly flapping its wings in the Amazon could be responsible for generating a storm in Aberdeen a year later. I can't say that knowing about Amazonian butterflies or the herding instinct in London buses does anything for me, but I am interested in how this might relate to the apparently random system of treasure hunting and finds recovery.

The treasure hunting press frequently reports of finds being made in quite peculiar circumstances. For example: I recently found my first pilgrims' ampulla, or holy water container, in thirty years treasure hunting. As I frequently search fields around Canterbury, home of one of the two major shrines in England (the other is Walsingham), I suppose I had to find such a relic eventually. But why after having a conversation on ampullae with a fellow enthusiast, one week before and being given a holy water receptacle in Valencia two weeks previously? And this was only one in a long string of similar occurrences going back almost to my first day treasure hunting.

My first recollection of these strange happenings was when using metal detectors back in the 1970s. Metal detectors had no discrimination circuits in those days although they had a "natural" insensitivity to some metals. I had two machines then, one was fairly insensitive to iron, loved aluminium foil and was good on inland sites; the other being oppositely inclined was good on the beach. One of the sites I wanted to search was a local park, which would be difficult for either machine owing to high levels of both foil and iron contamination.

Nevertheless I had a cunning plan, which was to use both detectors at the same time and only dig out finds where both machines had given a signal. I invited a friend, Steve, along to operate one detector, while I operated the other and walking side by side we cross-checked each other's signals. The system worked well producing better than a i:1 finds to junk ratio. After a while digging was becoming quite tedious using our somewhat inefficient garden trowel, and Steve said it would be a lot easier to extract the finds if we had brought along a screwdriver. Right on cue, the next find was an aluminium-handled screwdriver that had been pushed vertically into the ground. Not only was it a screwdriver but it was perfect for the intended task of probing for the object and flicking it out of the ground. This method of find extraction actually works better than it sounds for modern coins on parkland and is still popular in the USA, I understand, although I wouldn't recommend it in Britain as the odd coin you might damage will probably be gold.

At this time I preferred searching beaches and while there were days which produced a lot of the same denomination coin or type of jewellery, I always assumed this was due to tidal distribution . One incident I recall well, however, was my mother-in-law visiting and asking if I had found any silver threepenny pieces. I replied that I had only ever found one and that was many years before. Later that day I went off to the beach with my detector, switched on and immediately found a George V silver threepence.

I had not long taken to searching farmland, when, out for a run one Sunday morning, our dog lost the spherical bell she always wore on her collar. My wife, Sue, was quite upset about it because although these bells are inexpensive, actually getting a replacement was difficult at the time and I commented that it would be easier for me to go out and find a crotal bell, even though I had never found one before. I went metal detecting that same afternoon and, would you believe it, I found my very first crotal bell which was not only complete but in good working order and of similar size to the one lost.

Sometime later, after being dragged kicking and screaming into the computer age, we had a flatbed scanner installed on our PC. Solely with the intention of testing the scanner, I flicked through a treasure hunting magazine that was lying around and selected a page from an article about some lucky chap finding a small hoard of Ambiani Iron Age gold stater coins. Having a picture and text it was ideal for the purpose. The scanner produced a good copy, which I printed off, admired and left on my desk. The following day I went detecting on a chalky field, which had produced a fair amount of Roman material. As well as some 4th century coins I found a small heavy white disc, which I took to be lead. I started to gently wipe some of the chalk off and saw the outline of a horse on one side, which I thought was quite unusual for what I had almost decided was a token. Not totally convinced, I applied a bit of spittle that washed enough chalk away to expose gold and realised I had found an Ambiani stater, exactly the same type as in the article I had scanned the previous day. About a year later I started finding more Ambiani gold staters and have since equalled the number discussed in the article.

On another occasion, a farmer friend asked me to look for his lost penknife. I made a thorough search where the farmer believed he had lost his knife and turned up a useless rusty penknife. Over the next four weeks, every time I went out with my detector and regardless of where I went, I found at least one corroded penknife, ending up with six and not one of them any good. At this point I realised I had little chance of finding the lost item and gave the farmer a new Swiss Army knife I had left over from those halcyon days when sales representatives showered gifts on everyone they met. Would you believe, I haven't dug up a penknife since although I have experienced a spate of similar copycat finds.

On one farm I frequent, the farmer's wife took an interest in treasure hunting and uses my spare detector; sometimes accompanying me, occasionally going it alone. Considering she is inexperienced, using an obsolete detector and only puts in a small fraction of the time I spend treasure hunting, she is amazingly adept at turning up good finds. From a field, which was notable for its absence of medieval material, she unearthed her first medieval horse harness pendant complete with hanger. A very nice example it is too, showing the lions of England enamelled in red.

A week later, on another field, also notable for its lack of medieval finds, I found my first harness pendant of a different shape but also complete with hanger and having a lion enamelled in red. Not long after, my detecting partner found a nice medieval pendant cross, probably from horse-harness, which I rather admired so the following week I went out and found my own medieval cross. My partner then went for an action replay by finding another harness pendant on yet another field lacking in medieval finds, this one similar to the one I had found. I didn't manage to find my next pendant immediately it took a few weeks this time.

The beginning of 2002 heralded a new phase in copycat finds where I moved on to duplicating my own finds. It all started with me finding a modern copy of a Saxon key of a type which, I believe, was given away with a girls' comic about 50 years ago. The following week I found a medieval casket key on a different field and yet another the following week on a third site. The fourth week produced the final key of the series, or perhaps a winder, embossed with the name "Copydex", the well-known adhesive.

It couldn't have been more than a week or two later when I dug up a 13th century lead seal matrix inscribed in Latin "Thomas son of Henry". A few weeks later, up came a 14th century copper-alloy seal matrix, which once belonged to a merchant from Stanground, Cambridgeshire, also called Thomas. Some weeks later, on a club rally, I picked up a Georgian fob seal displaying a man's head. There is no legend and I don't know who the man was but it wouldn't surprise me if the name Thomas was involved somewhere.

Between finding the second and third seal matrices another club rally brought me a lovely 15th-16th century iconographic gold ring showing St Catherine and a male saint believed to be John the Baptist on the bezel with flowers and hearts around the hoop. While it pales into insignificance against the former example, which earned me a half share in a £3,750 ($7,500) Treasure award, I found a 9ct gold signet ring of 1940s vintage the following week.

With all this going on in a fairly short space of time it started the old grey matter working overtime. Looking back over the events described, most finds were, to borrow from Tolkein, "unlooked for", in as much as I wasn't seeking anything specific at the time. Exceptionally, the penknives turned up regularly from the time I started looking until I inadvertently removed the need to find any more and was arguably the most successful search of all. So would it be possible to "engineer" a specific type of find? I had no idea, but I had to give it a try.

For the trial I needed to pre-select something that was neither easy nor impossible to find and I settled for a hammered gold coin, which had eluded me for 30 years. It didn't really matter what the actual coin was so long as it fitted into the category, but I called the search my noble quest after the coin I most admired. I had certainly never heard of anyone actually achieving this, so had little idea of how to go about it other than a general feeling that I needed to do something rather than just leave it to chance. Drawing from other areas of experience I started by writing down my goal:

"I have found a hammered gold coin." Now according to the experts, if you set a goal you are supposed to read it out on a daily basis until it is achieved. I started doing this with all good intentions but soon stopped owing to other distractions and resorted to just having serious conversations with my metal detector on what it was supposed to be finding whenever I was out in the field.

Another ploy I tried was the old scanner trick: I scanned a picture of some medieval gold coins and kept the resulting image in my finds bag. That was fine until it rained and the scan turned into a soggy mess. In hindsight I should have had the scan laminated.

The third thing I did was to research and gain another (I already had one) deserted medieval manor site in the firm belief that if I was going to find hammered gold, I needed to search where there would have been people wealthy enough to have had such coins to lose. In the early part of the year conditions were right for searching this orchard site and I concentrated my efforts here. Hammered silver and some nice artefacts turned up including a near miss on a gold angel with a medieval gilded lead cherub and a 1920s wristwatch with its case made of the noble metal. However, by the time the hardening ground and developing fruit necessitated me abandoning the site for the summer, my goal had not been realised.

I shifted my searching to a ploughed field, which had produced medieval finds in the past, until August, when the wheat had been harvested on my other deserted medieval manor site. As seems to be the growing trend these days the farmer drilled a new crop into the stubble almost immediately, without ploughing, but was kind enough to allow me a month of searching on his emerging crop. Over the past few years that this site had been available to me, some really nice coins and artefacts had turned up, ranging in date from Roman through Saxon and medieval to Georgian and Victorian. Considering the site's previous record the next three weeks were quite disappointing as only a few fairly nondescript finds emerged and I wasn't hopeful of much more when I began searching on the fourth and final week of this season. My finds bag was all but empty after two hours, when a crisp signal produced a lovely medieval seal matrix with a squirrel design. I carried on searching, again finding little, until it was time to get myself home before my dinner ended up in the dog. I worked my way back towards my car, parked on the edge of the field, quite happy at having found the seal matrix. Five yards from the car my detector rang out a clear non-ferrous signal. I dug for the target and in the first spit of soil removed, I noticed a crumpled piece of gold foil. As I bent down to remove this junk from the field, I could see that it looked more substantial than foil and carried a design. I had a great deal of difficulty believing the object might be what I thought it was, but once I touched it I knew it was a hammered gold coin. I could not identify the coin there and then as it was folded in half, covered in dirt and I didn't have my spectacles. I checked, then filled in the hole and detected the last few yards to the car; there were no more signals so the coin had been the last find on the last search of this field, for this year at least. Back at the car I gently washed the coin in the dog bowl I carry, but even with my spectacles I did not recognise the design and thought it might be foreign. Back at home, however, my reference books told me my noble quest had ended with an English quarter noble of Edward III (left).

One swallow doesn't make a summer, so I picked another target, Saxon gold, and

repeated the exercise. Fairly soon after I found a 6th century gold pendant (right). I am now quite convinced that you can decide what you want to find and then go out and dig it up.

RESEARCH

No matter how good your dowsing is, it is vital that you do some research, for if you don't know what you are looking for with some degree of certainty then how can you hope to find it? You also need to identify the best potential sites as you might be spending hours on a field chasing a few Victorian sixpences when you could be finding a pot of gold coins on the next. It is true that dowsing allows you to be less precise with your research as you only need to identify what treasure you want to dowse for and its approximate location, for you can use your dowsing to home in with a fair degree of precision. The other great advantage of research is that you can use it to convince a landowner that there is something buried on his land and so hopefully gain search permission. In the absence of other evidence, very few people will accept a dowser's word that a treasure exists, so if you have to convince someone to give you permission or to supply resources then it is almost essential that you have some research to show them.

Research can take many forms and you should become involved in at least some of them. You can if you wish use dowsing to decide which form research should take – simply ask your pendulum or L-rod whether a particular form of research is the best one to use in your own case. Check all the possibilities and go with the YES answers. You can even select a book from a shelf or list and a page in a book in the same way if you want. Is this book the best one to use? Will this book tell me what I'm looking for? Is the information I want on page 100? Is the information before page 100? Is it after page 100? Etc.

By research you are, as a generalisation, trying to identify places where people in the past lived, worked, played and particularly where they might have lost valuables or buried their cash. Banks are a fairly recent innovation and many people never trusted banks anyway and still don't. As a dowser you have a great advantage over other treasure hunters because you can locate treasure from a distance. You only need a rough idea of where treasure might be, you do not need the precise details because you can lead yourself to the treasure. And don't forget to ask your rod or pendulum if the treasure has already been found or you could end up on a wild goose chase.

MAIN RESEARCH SOURCES

● **Other people's research on potential treasure sites**

In earlier years of treasure hunting in the UK there were numerous treasure site guides produced of which some are still around, particularly those written by Brian Cross. I have listed some in the bibliography. You might think that the sites have been thoroughly gone over but in my experience hardly anyone bothers with them, probably because they think everyone else has already beaten them to it. You should also bear in mind that even if a treasure exists it may not have been found. My own little Iron Age gold coin hoard eluded me for years and only turned up after the field was ploughed for the first time in a decade.

The only problem I found when I tried a selection of these sites was getting permission, mainly because nearly all the sites I looked at were owned by commercial organisations. (There was an Abbey treasure on land owned by a builder and an Iron Age treasure on land owned by a mining company, for instance.) But don't let that put you off, you only need one person to say yes to a request for search permission.

• Local History Books

There are a vast number of Local History books around, any of which may have leads to interesting sites. I am particularly fond of the older or so-called antiquarian histories as they give eyewitness accounts of places as they were 100-200 years ago or more. Titles that spring to mind are: Edward Hasted, *The History and Topographical Survey of the County of Kent.* John Nichols, *The History and Antiquities of the County of Leicester.* Robert Thoroton, *The Antiquities of Nottinghamshire.* Robert Surtees, *The History and Antiquities of the County Palatine of Durham.* John Edwin Cussans, *The History of Hertfordshire.* John Hutchins, *The History and Antiquities of the County of Dorset.*

An excellent place to start is *The Victoria County History* series, which began in the early years of the 20th century and covers most of England from prehistoric times to the Victorian era. In addition to the *Victoria History* most counties have at least one antiquarian who travelled the highways and byways writing about what he saw; what he was told and what he researched. Your local library is bound to have something along these lines.

The other county history series worth looking at are the Domesday Book translations inexpensively published by Phillimore which give an eyewitness account of England more than 900 years ago. These are particularly useful for finding Saxon sites such as lost settlements, mills and other buildings which could lead to rare and valuable Saxon treasures.

• Books on finding sites of various periods

These type of books tell you what features to look for to find treasures of various periods such as:

⌘ Water

Rivers, streams, springs, wells, ponds etc., were vital from ancient times to fairly recently. They supplied water for survival and rivers often supplied an efficient means of transport and power for mills. Iron Age people worshipped water gods making offerings in and around water sites. The Romans were in the habit of throwing coins into rivers whenever they crossed them and they sometimes buried caches around the point where a Roman road crossed a river. The Saxon's built watermills alongside rivers, which may have lasted well into medieval times. Trading would have taken place around these mills as the farmer had to pay the miller to grind his corn. Coins and other objects would have been lost, many of which could be very valuable today.

⌘ Roman Villas

There are thousands of villa sites all over the country. They will generally be scheduled and so out of bounds but the fields for up to a half a mile around will probably contain considerable Roman losses and possibly a hoard or two.

⌘ Churches

The church was the focal point of a community and there would have been fairs and other gatherings around old churches not to mention the possible hiding of the church's treasures from Henry VIII's plundering.

⌘ Places where caches have been previously found

Caches often turn up in multiples for at least a couple of reasons one being that hoarders would divide up their savings into two or three lots so they wouldn't lose all if someone discovered their hiding place. Another reason is that an event such as an imminent attack triggered off a spate of hoard burying by several people simultaneously.

• Local Knowledge

Never miss the opportunity of chatting to the older inhabitants of any place you may be interested in, they can often tell you snippets of information that will aid your searches. Also well worth tracking down is the, usually at least one, local historian who knows just about everything there is to know about a place. Don't forget farm workers either. They are usually very knowledgeable about matters relating to the land and will often surprise you with just what they do know. I'll never forget a casual labourer walking up to me while I was searching a site saying: "There was a Roman battle fought here, you know". According to one local historian he was absolutely right.

• Maps

Modern maps are essential for dowsing and subsequently finding what you have dowsed. The current popular Ordnance Survey maps are the *Landranger* at a scale of 1¼ inches to 1mile ~ 2cm to 1km and the old *Pathfinder* or new *Explorer* at double the scale i.e. 2½ inches to 1mile ~ 4cm to 1km. The larger scale *Pathfinder* or *Explorer* is much better for our purposes as it contains more detail. You can gain much information by comparing old maps with modern maps such as the sites of lost buildings, trackways, changed river courses etc.. Particularly useful for this purpose are the 6 inches to 1mile late Victorian or early twentieth century Ordnance Survey maps and the early nineteenth century reprints of the first series 1 inch to 1mile Ordnance Survey maps. The 6 inches to 1mile maps will be available at public libraries serving the area covered by the map or County Record Offices for the entire county. The first series 1 inch to 1 mile map reprints are produced by David and Charles, Newton Abbot, Devon and are available from many metal detector retailers.

Two other series of maps, which are excellent for research are enclosure maps and tithe maps which, between them cover almost every rural parish in England and Wales. These are large scale maps, typically 12 inches to the mile, showing every building and field in the parish. Every field or plot of land is numbered and by referring the field number to an associated index called the enclosure award or tithe apportionment we can find the name of the field, what its use was, its area, tenant and landowner. Particularly important for research is the name of the field from which we might, with care, gain some clues as to what went on there in the past. For instance a field called *Pennypot* probably gave up a cache of medieval pennies. I say 'with care' because *Penny Field* is more likely to refer to a rent payable of one penny. Your dowsing should sort the wheat from the chaff or consult a field name dictionary.

• Landscape Observation

Hedge boundaries might be evidence of earlier human activity. Plant species like blackthorn, holly and whych-hazel indicate centuries of human presence. Varying soil colours are evidence of previous habitation. Crop marks, produced by foundations reducing plant growth and ditches increasing plant growth, can indicate lost roads, buildings and settlements.

METAL DETECTORS

Regardless of how good your dowsing is, final pinpointing of the target for recovery can be difficult unless you use some sort of detecting device. In the case of non-metallic treasures there are few detecting devices available so you may have little choice but to dig until you find what you seek. In the case of recovering metallic treasures, however, there is an overwhelming array of metal detectors to choose from. If you already own a metal detector, then you have probably made a good choice and frankly any metal detector worth its name will perform the task of final target recovery. Not only that, your detector's performance should improve for it has been shown that any device, detector or instrument yields beyond normal results when used by a dowser.

For those of you who are not already detectorists I will make a few suggestions but the final choice of what to buy must be yours. I've lost count of the number of times I've heard the question: "Which metal detector is best?" The question should really be: "Which metal detector is best for me?" For the answer depends very much on you and your requirements.

• Do you want to mainly dowse and just have a metal detector for final recovery?
• Do you want to search for metal in places where you can't or don't want to dowse?
• Do you want to search beaches, rivers, farmland, underwater?
• Do you want to metal detect mainly and just dowse occasionally?

The vast majority of metal detectors are designed for finding coins, jewellery and similar sized artefacts in the top few inches of ground on inland sites while discriminating out the undesirable contaminants: iron and aluminium foil, for that is what most participants of the metal detecting hobby want. Iron is a major contaminant on farmland and aluminium foil abounds on beaches and recreational areas. Most popular machines work on a Very Low Frequency, Transmit/Receive system, discriminate audibly and/or visually and use the motion system of ground cancelling. Ground cancelling nulls effects from minerals in the ground and the motion system requires the machine to be kept moving otherwise desirable objects are also cancelled out. The system actually works a lot better than might be imagined. To pinpoint a target there is usually a selectable non-motion all metal mode although it is easy enough to pinpoint in motion mode by passing the head over the target in a cross pattern. Machines at the lower end of the market may be non-motion and may have little or no discrimination although by nature, these types are fairly insensitive to iron but very sensitive to aluminium foil.

TYPICAL 'SWITCH ON AND GO' MOTION DETECTOR

Within the motion detector range there are choices to be made regarding the desired amount of user control over the machine's electronic operation. Manufacturers are clearly split between simple 'switch on and go' and fully programmable detectors; some manufacturers making only one type and some making both types. Logically the computer controlled programmable type will be better able to maximise depth and discrimination but you could spend a great deal of time messing about with the settings trying to achieve perfection instead of searching. My own view is that if you are getting involved with dowsing then that will far outweigh any advantages of the computer control without the complexities but at the end of the day the choice is entirely yours. Whites have been the traditional UK choice for programmable types but Garrett, C-Scope and Minelab also offer programmable models.

A less popular type of hobby metal detector works on a principle known as pulse induction which is a non-motion deep seeking system. These machines are notoriously sensitive to iron and very few discriminate between ferrous and non-ferrous metals at all or at best poorly. Pulse machines are firm favourites among beachcombers and underwater treasure hunters because of their ability to reach greater depths on most targets, typically twice that of many VLF machines, and to cut through severe mineralisation such as black sand.

There are two types of very specialised machines generally available one being underwater detectors, which are sealed to keep out water and constructed to withstand the pressures encountered in deep water. The other speciality is the so-called hoard hunters, which are usually some sort of 'two-box' design, carried like a suitcase, rather than a forearm extension as with conventional detectors. Hoard hunters are designed to find only large objects, the size of a pint (565ml) pot upwards. They do not discriminate between ferrous and non-ferrous metals as treasure may be buried in an iron container (detectors cannot detect through metal) and they are very deep seeking, capable of probing several feet into the ground.

The standard coil size fitted to the majority of detectors is eight-inch diameter, which is a compromise to enable the detector to perform reasonably well under a variety of conditions. Most manufacturers produce a range of optional coil sizes typically from 3.5" (89mm) up to 15" (380mm) diameter and these can be used to improve performance under certain conditions. Generally the larger the coil the deeper it will detect but will be less sensitive to smaller targets, more difficult to use on heavily mineralised or iron contaminated ground and pinpoint less accurately. Larger coils are also heavier and more cumbersome, although the weight can be compensated for by hip mounting the detector control box if the machine allows.

In addition to size variation there are two different types of coil construction: concentric and 2D or widescan. Concentric coils, usually fitted to metal detectors as standard, have an inverted cone detection pattern, which achieves maximum depth only at the centre of the coil. Widescan coils have a pudding basin shaped detection pattern and while they don't achieve as great a depth as the same size concentric coil they do take in a larger volume of ground per sweep. If it's fast ground coverage you are after, the widescan coil is better and if it's depth you are after the concentric coil is better. If you have any choice in the matter, widescan is better for typical metal detector searching and concentric is better for locating dowsed targets.

CONCENTRIC & 2D
COIL DETECTION
PATTERN

THE CHOICES

The choice of machine, from over 150 models available, is very much dependent on what you want to do with it. If you just want a basic machine then go for one of the lower priced ones from your own Country. They are better value for money and probably more suitable for your conditions. Typically if you buy an American machine in Britain you pay pound on the dollar and the conditions and even the artefacts which are looked for are quite different in the two Countries. Amongst the higher priced detectors, foreign technology may be superior to your Country's and there may be less advantage in going for the home produced model. Foreign detectors made in Britain or for the British market have a large following. Laser and Whites particularly, with Minelab gaining ground.

If you mainly want to carry out searches with a metal detector and just use dowsing to assist then I would suggest you go for a detector in the middle to top price bracket. You can always buy second-hand to keep the cost down and detectors can keep going for many years. I know of a fifteen-year old Tesoro that is still in regular use. If you expect to search mainly inland then a VLF machine will be more suitable. If you want to search beaches then a pulse machine will probably be more suitable but bearing in mind the lack of discrimination on Pulse Induction machines, it may be preferable to go for a VLF machine with a good reputation on beaches such as Whites or Minelab.

Anyone spending a lot of time detecting usually has more than one metal detector. I personally have three:

- A Laser B1 Hi-Power as my main inland machine with a selection of coils – 3.5", 8" concentric, 8.5" widescan, 11" concentric, 11" widescan, 18" x 3.5" cleansweep. I use the Laser with the 8.5" widescan coil most of the time. I fit one of the 11" coils or the cleansweep for fast ground coverage on pasture with short grass or rolled arable and occasionally use the 3.5" for badly contaminated ground like river foreshores.

- A Minelab Sovereign XS2aPRO with 10" and 15" coils. I really bought this machine for seeking large deep targets using the 15" coil but have found the Minelab to be excellent on beaches and inland using the 10" coil.

CURRENT POPULAR METAL DETECTORS

NAME	ORIGIN	TYPE	PRICE RANGE
BOUNTY HUNTER	USA	VLF	£99-£349
C-SCOPE	UK	VLF/PULSE	£130-£650
FISHER	USA	VLF	£189-£699
GARRETT	USA	VLF	£169-£929
LASER (TESORO)	USA (FOR UK)	VLF	£339-£599
MINELAB	AUSTRALIA/EIRE	PULSE	£335-£2599
PULSEPOWER	UK	VLF	£699-£1200
TESORO	USA	VLF	£229-£695
VIKING	UK	VLF	£75-£245
WHITE'S	USA/UK	VLF/PULSE	£230-£849
XP	FRANCE	VLF	£299-£649

- A Pulsepower Goldscan II, which has an 11" coil, I use for beaches and deep-seeking work. Although the general advice is Pulse machines are not suitable inland, I use mine on some fields in conjunction with dowsing which eliminates most of the problems and capitalises on the Pulses depth capabilities.

I wouldn't suggest for one minute that my selection represents the absolute best in metal detecting technology but, in conjunction with dowsing, it does allow me to perform well over a wide variety of sites and conditions.

OTHER ASSOCIATED EQUIPMENT

HEADPHONES

Rather than being just an accessory, headphones are almost essential, for they allow you to hear the faintest of signals as well as cutting out any background noise. Hi-fi headphones are OK for short term use but if you want reliability and durability as well as good performance than you really need headphones which are made for use with metal detectors these cost around £40 upwards but are well worth the money.

DIGGING TOOLS

For normal detecting you need something which is strong and portable as you will need to carry it around with you, preferably on your person. A foot-assisted trowel is favourite, the bigger the better providing you can put up with having it attached to you. Ordinary garden trowels are pretty useless, being too small and weak. For dealing with a small number of deep targets, as you might if you are mainly dowsing, then you might need to use a few garden tools – spade, fork and pickaxe. Unless you are cache hunting you only tend to dig small holes – large holes take a long time to dig.

THE DEPTH DOUBLER

I have never been brave enough to try it but they say that when metal detecting in a thunderstorm or with a thunderstorm approaching, much greater depth is achieved. Unless you are planning an early retirement from this life, I don't recommend that you wave a metal detector around in thunderstorms. But you might consider a safer alternative called the Depth Doubler, which works independently of thunderstorms. This is an electronic device, which pumps an electric charge into the ground over a small area via a series of probes. The theory is that the electric charge attaches to buried metal objects making them appear larger to a metal detector and since, metal detectors detect large objects deeper than small ones, depth is increased, relative to the size of the object, up to twice normal. I have not used one and have read mixed reports of their effectiveness. They are somewhat awkward to use because you have to keep putting the probes into the ground and then pulling them out again to move to the next area that you want to search. Nevertheless, I can see that this device could be useful for maximising recovery from small areas such as you might define with dowsing.

PUTTING IT ALL TOGETHER

There are many claims of treasure finds through the use of dowsing although they tend to be abroad rather than in the British Isles and some have to be taken with a pinch of salt. To show you how it has been done by others I'm going to relate four accounts which I know to be true and can be proven, the first two concern Jim Longton's finds, the second two, my own. The basic formula for dowsing for treasure is fairly simple:

- Find a potential treasure site by research, experience or accident
- Dowse a map, chart or photograph of the site to check if the treasure exists and to find its approximate location
- Pinpoint the treasure using any means at your disposal
- Recover the treasure

The Penrith Hoard

In 1990 metal detectorist, William Carter, discovered by researching local histories, that one hundred years or more before, someone had found a silver Viking brooch in a field, not far from his home. The field was called *Silver Field*. Realising that there might be more silver remaining in the ground, William contacted Jim Longton and asked him to dowse a map of the field. Jim dowsed the map and announced that there was indeed more silver scattered over a circle, one hundred metres in diameter. The two of them contacted the landowner and explained their findings. Permission to search the field was granted. Jim used his dowsing rod to pinpoint the hotspots, marking them with flags, while William used his metal detector to check for metal. Their final haul, handed in to their local museum under the former treasure trove practice, consisted of six brooches - three intact and three in pieces. The British Museum retained the brooches and an award of £42,200 ($84,000) was shared between the finders and landowner.

The Secret Treasure of Charles I

Almost everyone knows that Charles I, the only British Monarch to be executed by his subjects, lost his head but very few know that he also lost a vast treasure, not once, but twice! The second treasure was melted down by Cromwell and largely consisted of an expensive replacement for the first, lost in Scotland's Firth of Forth in 1633.

In 1625 Charles I was crowned King of England but Scotland was a separate Kingdom and Charles also had to be crowned there. It was eight years before the King set off for his Scottish Coronation departing London on 10 May 1633 with an entourage of 150 English Lords, royal guards, servants and baggage. Travelling overland, the King arrived in Edinburgh nearly five weeks later to be crowned in the Abbey Church of Holyrood on Tuesday 18 June 1633.

It was customary for the Monarch to carry his personal finery with him so that he could entertain and be entertained in the manner to which he was accustomed. Amongst his baggage was a 230 piece silver gilt service from which a string of earlier monarchs had dined. As his Coronation tour began the King was showered with expensive gifts from his Scottish subjects, which grew as the days went by. The planned itinerary was to last well into July visiting Linlithgow, Sterling, Dunfermline, Falkland and back to Edinburgh. At Falkland the King cut short his stay to make an unscheduled visit to Perth where he had arranged a highland gathering to entertain the party. But the King was growing tired and anxious to return to London.

On the morning of 9th July the King was back at Falkland Palace where his staff made ready for the journey home. At 3am the following day, in deteriorating weather conditions, the King and major entourage with the most valuable baggage, left for Burntisland ferry to take the shortest route back to Edinburgh across the Firth of Forth. His Majesty's warship, *The Dreadnought,* having sailed from London as part of the supply train, anchored off the harbour awaiting to transport the party in reasonable comfort across the water to Edinburgh's port of Leith. The King was transferred to *The Dreadnought* by pinnace but the ferry-boat following behind, *The Blessing of Burntisland,* heavily laden with baggage-wagons, was caught in a sudden squall, keeled over and sank. Of the 35 men on board the ferry, only two survived.

The loss of the Royal baggage and many friends was sad and embarrassing for Charles. He changed his plan of returning to London on *The Dreadnought* and travelled overland, either so all could see he was still alive and well or to avoid the sea, or both. Later, perhaps to avoid the Scottish clergy interpreting the loss as "an act of God", a group of Lancashire witches were executed for the sinking and the whole episode passed into obscurity.

In the 1980's, Robert Brydon, a top historical researcher in Edinburgh, stumbled upon the story. As the story took shape, Bob realised that apart from the historical interest he had probably found the key to the greatest treasure loss in Britain. Bob was keen to search for the lost ferry. Unfortunately all his contacts who could have assisted him were engaged in other projects.

The search was shelved until 1991 when Bob met up with Howard Murray a leading marine conservationist who had worked on the recovery of Henry VIII's ship, the *Mary Rose.* Howard was intrigued by the story and contacted his friend Martin Rhydderech, another historical researcher. They spent several weeks going over Bob's work and eventually found a new piece of information detailing all the silverware that had to be replaced following Charles' Scottish coronation – about half a tonne!

Now that they had definite proof that the treasure had been lost they only had to find it! But difficult conditions in the Firth of Forth meant it wasn't going to be easy. Poor underwater visibiltiy and strong currents made searching for a wreck buried deep in the mud, an expensive and time consuming prospect needing more resources than Howard and Martin had.

Local entrepreneur Alec Kilgour then became involved. He managed to persuade the Forth Ports Authority to provide a survey vessel and British Gas to provide some revolutionary undersea oil exploration equipment. Bentech, a Norwegian Company, also chipped in by lending a sonar system. All through the summer of 1992 the team scoured the Forth for wrecks. By the end of the summer they had identified over 200 targets in the two square mile search area which historical research had defined.

The next stage was to check each target out with divers but winter was beginning and they were almost out of funds. They attempted to find investors but investors wanted to sell any treasure recovered, which didn't fit in with the team's plan of conservation and display.

Alec then read of a similar project in the States. Barry Clifford, a professional treasure hunter had discovered the *Whydah,* an 18th century pirate galleon buried in mud in only 30 feet of water. Alec contacted Barry and that summer (1993) the search really began. Barry and his team of American divers occasionally aided and abetted by Prince Andrew and the Royal Navy investigated many of the targets. But despite a diligent search lasting three years, they failed to find anything earlier then the 18th century and went home.

The search all but dried up during 1996 but in 1997 a friend of Alec Kilgour named Ian Archibald contacted the original team and the search recommenced. Apart from his diving and map skills, Ian knew dowser Jim Longton and although sceptical went to Lancashire to see him. Jim dowsed some charts with the pendulum and later travelled to Burntisland for a spot of 'field' dowsing. Ian took Jim out in a dive boat and navigated by pointing the boat in the direction indicated by Jim's dowsing rod. Suddenly, Jim's rod started swinging wildly, out of control. They stopped the boat and Ian was amazed to discover they were within a few metres of the spot Jim had marked on the chart, in fact Jim was more accurate than a satellite positioning system. Jim was also amazed, as he had not experienced the rod's wild gyrations before. He now believes the rod followed the course of the *Blessing of Burntisland* as it ran into trouble all those years ago.

Several months later Ian was able to verify a wreck of the right dimensions and the right age right at the spot Jim indicated. Diving is extremely difficult, with the tides only allowing 20 minutes access daily and the wreck is deep in the mud. A few pieces of 17th century pottery have been brought up, some with the name Longton on it. Everyone involved believes they have found King Charles' treasure ship but it has yet to be confirmed. Perhaps if they had started with a dowser in the first place instead of waiting six years we would all know for sure.

Valerian I Antoninianus 253-60

The Roman Dump

Brian, a fellow member of my detecting club who has fallen in with the aristocracy, searches land, which adjoins my favourite farm. Consequently, we both take a keen interest in what each other is finding and where. A while back, Brian was asked to look for a pair of Jacobean pistols which were supposed to have been hidden somewhere in the landowner's house. At the club meeting following his search, Brian said to me: "I was over at her Ladyship's place the other day, looking for those pistols I told you about. You'll never guess what I found." "You found the pistols." I replied. "No I didn't", said Brian, "But I found a cupboard full of Roman stuff with a letter from an archaeologist saying that it came from those fields you go on. You know, the ones her Ladyship used to own, years ago." "You're pulling my leg! I've spent hours and hours over there and all I've got to show for it is the finest collection of shotgun cartridge ends known to man." "Well, the archaeologist called it a Roman dump. It's there somewhere, you'll just have to find it."

'This is a job for Jim Longton', I thought and sent him a map of the farm. When the map came back, Jimmy had successfully identified areas where I had already found numerous coins and artefacts and had placed the Roman "dump" in a small copse. I tried to search the copse but it was too dense and I abandoned it without success. There was, however, a small field next to the copse which had defied being searched twice before, owing to inch thick kale stubble on the first occasion and frozen ground the second.

As luck would have it, I had no sooner given up on the copse when the farmer ploughed this small field. I started searching as close to the copse as I could get and was soon holding a Roman coin. By the time the field was drilled the total finds amounted to over forty Roman coins, a medieval ring and several other artefacts.

A few months later, after the field was ploughed again, I was rewarded with my first gold stater as well as more Roman coins and a Roman brooch. Okay, I admit the finds aren't spectacular but without map dowsing they would almost certainly still be in the ground.

Gold for the Gods

Although Jim Longton, Frank Delamere and myself had dowsed maps of a particular farm, we all failed to identify the potential at one end. The problem, I think, was an abundance of targets at the other end of the farm which kept me busy digging for a couple of years and yielded handfuls of Roman coins as well as other interesting coins and artefacts from the last two thousand years. Jim believes that the problem was that we were so focussed on Roman we only dowsed for Roman.

Research had shown a possible Roman road running through the farm but little else. The dowsing did show up one thing though and that was that the targets lay mainly along a riverbank, which skirted several of the fields. And that was where I found most of the metal objects. I concentrated on searching along the river bank whether map dowsing had shown targets or not and while the most productive area in terms of quantity had already been found by map dowsing, a few nice pieces came up from parts where map dowsing hadn't shown anything. Such was the case with one small field at the end of the farm, which had been pasture for many years. Under pasture identifiable finds dated no earlier than medieval but the plough soon changed that.

Much to my chagrin at the time, the day the field was ploughed and rolled the farmer walked across the field and plucked a single Iron Age gold coin from the ground. The condition was almost as minted, which suggested there might be more especially considering that the field sloped gently down to a ditch that had once held an impressive ring of bright water – a classic contender for a Celtic sacred site where offerings might be made to their gods. The farmer showed me where he had found the coin and I searched carefully around the find spot with a metal detector. Dowsing doesn't work well on freshly ploughed fields because of remanence, so I pretty well searched the whole field with the metal detector over the next few weeks until the growing crop forced me to stop. The only two finds worth mentioning amounted to an Elizabeth I sixpence and a Scottish four pence piece of David II, both about fifteen hundred years later than the Iron Age.

The crop had been harvested for more than a month and I hadn't set foot on the field until the farmer asked why I didn't go and have another look. 'The weeds are knee high' I thought: 'And what's more, I've already searched every square inch.' The question sounded somewhat rhetorical however, so saying "What a good idea!" I made my way to the field. 'Good idea indeed!' I thought as I struggled through the undergrowth making my way to the far side of the field where the farmer had found his coin. I eventually reached the spot the richer for one piece of lead and a fly button. As I turned at the field boundary, I noticed a relatively clear piece of ground a few metres away and headed for that. Just as I reached the patch a crisp signal stopped me in my tracks. I took out a trowelful of earth to be greeted by a gleaming gold disc lying on top of the little black spoil heap. I knew it was an Iron Age coin before I had even picked it up and amazingly within the hour I was holding a second gold coin. It was quite some minutes before I had recovered from the shock enough to carry on detecting.

I returned the next day for another go but the success of the previous day was not to be repeated. I had, however, brought a Polaroid SX-70 camera with me. As sunset approached, I set the camera and stood in the centre of a mentally described circle that surrounded the find spots of the three gold coins. I took the first shot of the lower part of the field where I had found the two coins and then stood staring at the developing print as bright yellow streaks formed around the find spots. I turned around and took another shot of the upper part of the field where the first coin had been found and saw five separate streaks develop, fainter than the previous print but definite nevertheless. These pictures seemed to indicate that there was more gold waiting to be found. That night, I sent copies of the photos to Frank Delamere, my dowser friend in Dublin, to see what he made of them.

The following day I was back on the field with an arsenal of deeper seeking devices: an 11-inch searchcoil on my *Laser,* my *Goldscan* pulse induction detector and my dowsing rod. I selected the *Goldscan* and set about the field, going over the find spots. I was quite surprised at the quantity of non-ferrous metal that emerged although a little disappointed that none was gold.

It was another week before I was able to return to the field. During the week, Frank returned my Polaroids annotated with crosses. Frank had dowsed the pictures and come up with some interesting results. In addition to accurately predicting the find spots of the three gold coins already found, Frank suggested a total of seven gold coins, two silver coins and a hoard of gold artefacts remained unrecovered

I continued searching over the following few weeks but nothing significant turned up until finally the plough returned. As if mocking all my previous effort, half an hour after searching the freshly ploughed field I was holding gold coin number four. The next two sessions produced no precious metal and I was beginning to believe that the field only gave up its gold on the initial search after ploughing or harvesting. Christmas was now upon us and I took some time out to study the dowsed Polaroids. The last coin I had found was just outside the shot and the predicted finds were scattered randomly over a quarter of an acre. Instead of concentrating around the areas immediately around the previous finds as I had been, I thought it would be worthwhile to investigate the predicted find spots one by one.

An hour into the search on Boxing Day I recovered coin number five. At the start of my next search, on the second day of the new Millennium, I was a little perturbed to hear crackling noises in my headphones as I switched my detector on but dismissed it as arcing from an electric fence. It was approaching dusk with almost nothing in my finds bag when I noticed that a piece of brass scrap I had just passed the coil over, failed to produce a signal. I unplugged the headphones and scanned the brass to check the detector, which reassuringly gave a clear signal. I continued detecting expecting to go home with nothing for my foolishness in not spotting the headphone problem earlier but the Gods were forgiving that day for the last signal pointed out a gleaming gold crescent; the edge of coin number six just breaking the surface. Before I had to abandon the field to the crop yet again, I added one more coin to the score, making the total a magnificent seven.

Occasionally things happen which defy belief. The next time the field was ploughed the farmer walked across the field and plucked another gold coin from the ground. I visited the field a couple of days later and within half an hour I spotted that unmistakable glint in the bottom of the hole. I knew the score before I picked the find up – farmers: 2, dowsers: 7…

TREASURE HUNTING BASICS

Professional treasure hunters, although very few in number, have been around for centuries. Generally they mounted extensive search and recovery operations costing large sums of money well beyond the reach of the average man or woman. The invention of the Aqua-lung by Jacques Yves Cousteau opened up the world of undersea exploration and wreck hunting to many, however locating and salvaging a potential treasure wreck, would still be very costly. It takes much silver to look for gold it used to be said.

The development of the hobby metal detector in the USA in the 1960s, changed all that and spawned popular treasure hunting. The new breed of treasure hunters in the USA, tend to search for relatively modern coin and jewellery losses on beaches and other recreational areas with the minority searching ghost towns, battle sites and for native gold. The hobby quickly spread to Britain where it is more popularly and less brashly called Metal Detecting and initially followed the same pattern of searching recreational areas. It was soon discovered that the farmland of Britain is relatively rich in lost metalwork from the last 2000-3000 years and in view of the greater interest and potentially greater reward for effort expended, most detectorists have migrated to the fields on a more or less permanent basis.

While probably not practised to such a great extent as in Britain and the USA, treasure hunting has spread to other parts of the world. In Australia gold nugget hunting is popular. Holland seems to be the only other keen participant in Europe although this may be as a result of constraints imposed by law in many countries. In Southern Ireland for instance it is not illegal to use a metal detector but it is illegal to use a detector to search for archaeological objects. And if you use a metal detector, you are presumed to be searching for archaeological objects! The only way round this is to convince the authorities that you are not searching for archaeological objects – whether a claim that you dowsed the site beforehand and found it to be free of archaeological objects would stand up in court, I don't know.

Fortunately in Britain although we do have the Treasure Act to contend with (of which more later) the situation is much better providing we follow a few simple rules set out by the hobby's main body, The National Council For Metal Detecting. You will find their code of conduct on the next page.

It's not my job to pontificate, however I do urge you to follow the code of conduct for you own sake and the sake of the hobby. There is nothing in the code that isn't either common courtesy or common sense and you could get yourself into serious trouble by ignoring it, not necessarily just from the law either.

Treasure Hunting is not a dangerous hobby if followed sensibly but venturing into unknown territory could be, as an acquaintance of mine will testify. While detecting in a park where he didn't have permission (many would argue that he didn't need permission but I think it's always best to ask) he unearthed two glass vials with brass tops. Unrecognised, they ended up in his car along with other finds until, on the way home, the action of rolling around dislodged some of the dirt and he noticed they were marked "War Department." He took them to the Police. The Police called the Bomb Squad who identified them as nitro-glycerine before safely detonating them. The resulting explosion was heard ten miles away! Had he sought permission he might have been forewarned of the possible dangers.

THE NATIONAL COUNCIL FOR METAL DETECTING CODE OF CONDUCT

- Do not trespass. Ask permission before venturing onto any private land.

- Respect the Country Code. Do not leave gates open when crossing fields and do not damage crops or frighten animals.

- Do not leave a mess. It is perfectly simple to extract a coin or other small object buried a few inches under the ground without digging a great hole. Use a sharpened trowel or knife to cut a neat flap (do not remove the plug of earth entirely from the ground), extract the object, replace the soil and grass carefully and even you will have difficulty in finding the spot again.

- Help to keep Britain tidy and help yourself. Bottle tops, silver paper and tin cans are the last things you should throw away. Do yourself and the community a favour by taking the rusty iron and junk you find to the nearest litter-bin.

- If you find any live ammunition or any lethal object such as an unexploded bomb or mine, do not touch it. Mark the site and report the find to the local police and landowner.

- Report all unusual historical finds to the landowner.

- Familiarise yourself with the law relating to archaeological sites. Remember it is illegal for anyone to use a metal detector in a protected place unless permission has been obtained from the appropriate Secretary of State or designated Authority. A protected place is defined in the Ancient Monuments and Archaeological Areas Act 1979.

- Acquaint yourself with the definitions of Treasure contained in the Treasure Act 1996 and its associated Code of Practice, making sure you understand your responsibilities if you find Treasure. Also, acquaint yourself with the definition and practice of Treasure Trove and the special circumstances in which it will now be applied.

- Remember that when you are out with your metal detector you are an ambassador for our hobby. Do nothing that may give it a bad name.

- Never miss an opportunity to show and explain your detector to anyone who asks about it. Be friendly. You could pick up some useful clues to another site. If you meet another detector user, introduce yourself. You may learn much about the hobby from each other.

GAINING SEARCH PERMISSION

There is no guaranteed way to obtain search permission and if you have your own way that works you should stick with it. Here is the method I prefer:

- Do a little research to find out something about the land, which is written down somewhere. The more information you can find, the better. It doesn't even matter if the information appears to be total rubbish (you don't know whether it is until you investigate). Copy the information and take down the references (i.e. Author, Title, Place and Year of Publication).

- Next, find out the name and title of the landowner from the telephone directory, Yellow Pages, the Electoral Register (copies in most town libraries) or local knowledge.

- Write (handwriting is fine as long as it is legible) a letter, discussing your research, along the lines of the following sample:

Your name
Your address
Your telephone number
Your email address (if you have one)

(Date)

(Landowner's Initial) *(Landowner's Surname)* Esq.
(Landowner's Address)

Dear *(Title e.g. Mr)* *(Surname)*,

Several years ago (name of local farmer, farm, Parish), kindly gave me permission to use a metal detector on his land. The finds recovered, from the top few inches of soil (coins, tokens, buttons, buckles and a variety of other metal artefacts that had been lost, hidden or discarded over the past 2000 years) led me to develop a considerable interest in the history of the area.

During the course of research I have come across several references to a Roman road that is supposed to have run through (name) parish. According to major sources (e.g. Ordnance Survey Map of Roman Britain) the road ran from the Iron Working area of (name) through (name) to (name), where it crossed the river and travelled up the East side to (name).

As the course of this road may have run through (name) Farm, I approached Mr. (name) for permission to detect on

his land (which he kindly gave), with a view to finding
the road. Having searched for some time and uncovered
much evidence of Roman and medieval finds to the east of
the river and having made a not inconsiderable number of
such finds to the west of the river; it looks highly
probable that the road continued on from (name) to (name)
Street, crossing your land. It is, perhaps, worth noting
that Roman finds have been made on nearly all adjoining
fields and that *street,* as in (name) Street, is a Roman
name.

I would greatly appreciate having your permission to use
a metal detector on your land with a view to determining
the course of the Roman road.

In return for your kind permission, I would offer to:

Report all worthwhile finds and findings to you.

Share any finds or their value with you on the
customary 50/50 basis.

Work tidily without leaving a mess; removing all junk
uncovered.

Respect your property and take care to avoid causing
damage, loss or hindrance (I have N.F.U./C.L.A.
approved Public Liability Insurance).

Abide by any conditions that you may wish to impose.

I am at your disposal should you require further
information or a demonstration and look forward to your
reply.

Yours Sincerely,

(*Your Signature*)

(*Your Name*)

- If you have produced the letter on a word processor save it. Otherwise make a copy of the letter and keep it.

- Enclose a stamped self-addressed envelope and copies of maps and any other printed material that supports your argument for wanting to search the land. Indicate on the map where you want to search if it isn't obvious.

- Post the letter and wait. You will often get a fairly quick yes. If you haven't heard from the landowner by the end of four weeks, visit him, if possible, taking a copy of your letter and research with you. You are not 'cold calling' so he should be approachable and he is unlikely to be completely against the idea or he would already have replied to that effect. You will just have to try and convince him to say yes even if it is only for a short probationary period.

- If you can't get to see the landowner send another brief letter suggesting you think the first may have been lost in the post and enclose a copy of the original letter with copies of everything you originally sent, including a stamped self-addressed envelope.

SEARCH AGREEMENTS

As money will probably be involved at some time during your searches, and disputes often arise over money, I advise you to try and get a signed, written search agreement at the outset. I have to say that landowners tend not to want to get involved with such things and I have only once succeeded in getting one drawn up myself. However, the written request for permission just outlined, includes an offer to share the proceeds equally. I don't pretend to be a lawyer but I am fairly sure that, in the event of a dispute, the copy of your letter you have kept together with any written permission from the landowner would stand up as evidence of an agreement. I am sure I don't need to tell you to play fair with landowners, for their goodwill is essential to your pursuit of treasure.

In case you can get a landowner to sign an agreement, on the following page there is an example you may copy and use:

LANDOWNER/SEARCHER AGREEMENT

The following terms and conditions are agreed between landowner and searcher:

The landowner grants permission to the searcher to use location equipment and hand tools to search and extract finds from the ground of land known as:
....
....

During the period: **From:**...**To:**...

The searcher enters the land at the searcher's own risk.

The searcher shall report all worthwhile finds to the landowner within a reasonable time of being found in accordance with the landowner's wishes.

The searcher shall report any bombs, missiles or live ammunition discovered, to the landowner and to the police.

Archaeological discoveries will be reported to the landowner in the first instance. The information will then be passed on to the local museum or archaeological body providing the landowner agrees.

Potential treasure discoveries will be reported to the landowner in the first instance providing this can be achieved within fourteen days. In any event the Coroner will be informed within fourteen days as prescribed by The Treasure Act.

All finds (or the value thereof) and treasure awards will be shared equally between the searcher and landowner.

The searcher shall take great care to: work tidily, avoid hindrance to the working of the land and avoid damage to the landowner's, property, animals or crops. In the unlikely event of damage the searcher shall rectify the damage at the searcher's own expense.

The searcher shall comply with any special conditions, recorded overleaf.

This agreement may be terminated by the landowner at any time and if so terminated the searcher shall immediately cease all operations.

	SEARCHER	LANDOWNER
SIGNATURE:	....	....
NAME:	....	....
ADDRESS:	....	....
	....	....
	....	....
DATE:	....	....

LIVING WITH THE TREASURE ACT

At present, treasure is defined, under the Act, as any object other than a coin, at least 300 years old when found, which has a metallic content, of which at least 10% by weight is gold or silver. And all coins that contain at least 10% by weight of gold or silver that come from the same find consisting of at least two coins, at least 300 years old. And all coins that contain less than 10% by weight gold or silver that come from the same find consisting of at least ten coins at least 300 years old. And any associated objects, except unworked natural objects (e.g. a pot or other container), found in the same place as treasure objects. And any objects or coin hoards less than 300 years old, made substantially of gold and silver that have been deliberately hidden with the intention of recovery and for which the owner is unknown. From 1 January 2003 the definition of treasure has been extended on prehistoric (i.e. up to the end of the Iron Age) finds to include all multiple artefacts, made of any metal, found together and single artefacts deliberately containing any quantity of precious metal.

The Act applies to objects found anywhere in England, Wales and Northern Ireland, including in or on land, in buildings (whether occupied or ruined), in rivers and lakes and on the foreshore (the area between mean high water and mean low water) providing the object does not come from a wreck. If the object has come from a wreck then it will be subject to the salvage regime that applies to wreck under the Merchant Shipping Act 1995. The Receiver of Wreck (located via Customs & Excise) must legally be notified of all property recovered following the loss of a vessel; and the salvor is entitled to a reward related to the value of the object, either from the owner, if identified, or the Crown.

If you are searching in other parts of the British Isles or outside of Britain altogether, you should familiarise yourself with treasure law for your specific area. In Scotland, for instance, all ownerless objects belong to the Crown. They must be reported regardless of where they were found or of what they are made. The finder receives market value as long as no laws have been broken. Not all finds will be claimed. Further information from: TTAP Secretariat, Archaeology Dept., National Museum of Scotland, Queen Street, Edinburgh, EH2 1JD.

I have the experience of having had to report seven separate finds of treasure since the introduction of the Treasure Act. There is little wrong with the Treasure Act itself but problems can arise when the Code of Practice isn't followed. My major concern is the lack of confidentiality promised regarding the findspot, for it seems that a number of Coroners have given away fairly precise details of findspots to the Press. For the benefit of novices the implication is that if thieves, usually called 'Nighthawks', learn the location of your site they may raid it in the hope of finding more treasure and may cause serious damage to the landowner's crops or other property in the process. You wouldn't blame the landowner if he then banned you from his land with his neighbours probably following suit. Painting the blackest picture, you could lose access to vast tracts of land and countless other treasures.

You are probably thinking if that is what could happen when you comply with the law you'll keep quiet when you find treasure. Unfortunately the penalty for not reporting is far greater, for if you get caught; you may be fined up to £5000 and be imprisoned for three months. You are then branded a criminal, which could seriously ruin your life.

But things are not as bad as they may look, mostly good things come from your honesty, like access to the next site and your next treasure find. The problems can be overcome if you know how. And you will know how by the time you've finished reading this chapter.

My first treasure find, in February 1999, was a gilt silver medieval ring brooch, unfortunately missing its sword-shaped pin, inscribed with the letters XIESVS (Christ Jesus) found, in close proximity to two contemporary silver coins. The findspot, on the site of a medieval Hundred Court, was near the boundary between two Coroners' provinces. It took three weeks to get one of them to accept responsibility as the Coroner's Officers were out most of the time and didn't return calls.

I was asked to deposit the find with a choice of three or four fairly local museums. I chose the most convenient to me and I am pleased to say the curator was very helpful. The landowner was on holiday at the time of the find and I arranged to delay depositing the items with the museum until the landowner had the opportunity to view them. When I deposited the objects in April, the curator advised putting a four-figure Ordnance Survey map reference on the Treasure Receipt and recorded the eight-figure reference separately.

The Museum didn't want to acquire the finds and after reference was made to the landowner, they were disclaimed and returned to me without fuss or publicity on 17 September 1999.

The second find began on the site of a Domesday water mill, in April 1999, with the finding of a single Ambiani type E Iron Age gold stater by the landowner. This coin didn't qualify as treasure by itself and wasn't reported. On September 30, 1999, I found two more Ambiani gold staters in the same place and reported all three to the Coroner about 12 days later. (I knew who the Coroner was this time.)

Because of the difficulties of my getting to a museum (at my own expense), we arranged for the finds to be deposited by the landowner at a different museum to the previous find. Based on advice previously received, I briefed the landowner on what information to put on the Treasure Receipt. With the agreement of the landowner, the curator filled in both the Treasure Receipt and the museum's standard receipt, recording eight-figure findspots together with the name of the farm on both receipts. The landowner was given the museum receipt and we were both later sent copies of the official Treasure Receipt.

During December 1999 and early January 2000, I recovered four more Ambiani staters, one by one from the same place (shown on front cover). I reported each one to the Coroner within 14 days of each find and the four were handed over to the Museum on 10 January 2000 by the landowner. The dual receipting procedure was repeated although in answer to the landowner's comments about terms on the museum receipt, which couldn't be applied to potential treasure finds, the curator crossed out the disagreeable parts.

The inquest was originally scheduled for late January but was postponed to 24 February as a result of the additional finds. The inquest was a quiet affair with only myself, landowner, Coroner and two officers in attendance. The coins were inevitably declared 'Treasure', the museum having an interest in acquiring them. Expenses were offered for attending court.

The Coroner's officer phoned the following day to tell me that the local Press wanted to speak to me, he also told me that he was legally obliged to reveal details of the find to the Press. I had discussions with the landowner who wanted no publicity. We decided that it would be better to speak to the Press and appeal to them not to reveal sensitive information, rather than risk them making their own stories up from what they got from the Coroner's office. While one reporter made it clear that he knew the landowner's name and the name of the farm, he did act responsibly and complied with our wishes to publish neither.

The Curator took the coins to the British Museum. We (landowner and myself) then received a letter from the Department of Culture Media and Sport (who administer the Treasure Act) saying the coins were being valued, the valuation would be sent to us and we would have 28 days to comment and offer alternative valuations. I did actually attempt to obtain a couple of valuations but could only get ballpark figures without the valuers being able to view the actual coins. One dealer requested £50 for this service but subsequently gave me a free retail valuation.

On 11 May I received a letter from the Department of Culture Media and Sport with a valuation report from Sotheby's (£1260-£1400). The letter said that the valuation committee was sitting the following day and we were not going to be allowed to make representations on the provisional valuation owing to Public holidays.

On 16 May the Department of Culture Media and Sport advised that the committee had valued the coins at £1350 and we had one month to make representation if dissatisfied. The Museum was also allowed to make representation on the valuation. The Museum then had up to four months to settle, from the time this figure was accepted by all parties. We agreed to accept the valuation, which was close to the ballpark figures given by the dealers.

Discussing this case with Bob Whalley, Co-ordinator for Policy, National Council for Metal Detecting, it came to light that the first coin found by the landowner should not have been declared Treasure as it was only a single find at the time. The Department of Culture Media and Sport agreed. The museum wanted all seven coins to maintain the integrity of the supposed hoard, however by request the coin was returned to the landowner and an agreed pro rata award, split equally between the landowner and myself, was made for the other six coins during October 2000.

After the autumn ploughing the landowner and myself found a further Ambiani stater each on the same field. I reported these to the Coroner within the stipulated 14 days and suggested we delayed handing the coins over until I had carried out further searching. As it happened, I didn't find any more, so the landowner took the two coins to the museum in mid-January 2001. The museum wanted these coins to add to the other six so they inevitably were going to be declared treasure. I was quite puzzled why the museum even wanted the coins in the first place, as Ambiani staters must be the most common Iron Age gold coins. In answer to that question the curator told me that they needed to keep them together for posterity and future research when improved analytical techniques may be able to provide more information.

Between January and the Inquest in May, the Coroner and his two officers all retired leaving a Deputy Coroner and a new officer to take charge of the case. As the inquest was suggested by the Coroner's officer to be just a brief formality, neither the landowner nor myself attended. The following day the Coroner's officer rang the landowner saying that the coins had been declared treasure and the Press had been given details, including the Landowner's telephone number. The Landowner was not happy, I was not happy and the following week when a report on the find appeared in the local paper, giving the full name and address of the mixed arable and dairy farm, in the midst of the Foot and Mouth crisis, we were livid. Locally there was not much that could be done other than to ask neighbours to look out for intruders, while Bob Whalley and I moved into written complaint mode. Bob wrote to the Deputy Coroner while I tackled Doctor Roger Bland, Adviser on Treasure. We eventually received replies from Doctor Bland, the Deputy Coroner and from two other Coroners who had each inherited part of the retired Coroner's area owing to a County reorganisation. The deputy Coroner said it wasn't anything to do with her any longer and couldn't comment, while one of the 'new' Coroners said she only referred to find spots by map reference. The second 'new' Coroner, on the other hand, while suggesting that information was given to the Press during the inquest, somewhat more encouragingly confirmed that her officers should not report findspots to the Press and promised to check out other possible sources of 'leaks', such as the Police Press Office.

Meanwhile the valuation was set at £440 for the two coins that the Deputy Coroner had determined had both been found by me and my attempts to rectify that verdict have fallen on deaf ears. The landowner and myself accepted the award, which was paid in January 2002, split 75% in favour of the landowner (I couldn't really claim half the value of a coin I didn't find).

In June 2002 on a club search in the grounds of a medieval manor house I found, within ten minutes, a fifteenth century iconographic gold finger ring engraved with figures of Saint Catherine, a bearded male believed to be Saint John the Baptist and floral motifs (shown on front cover). This clearly had to be reported to the Coroner. Aware of the recent reorganisation in the County, I wrote to the most likely candidate from the Treasure Act Code of Practice book and asked that my letter be passed to the appropriate Coroner if that office no longer dealt with the parish where I had found the ring. My letter was passed on to another Coroner who turned out to be the lady who only refers to the findspot by map reference.

I was asked to take the ring to the museum, which had dealt with the Staters and we went straight for the Treasure Receipt this time. I only gave a four-figure map reference for the findspot to be entered on the Treasure Receipt even though the Curator wanted six. I explained why I didn't want the full findspot reference recorded on the receipt and offered it to be kept separately although that was declined for the moment. The local museum wanted the ring so it went to Treasure Inquest, which unfortunately was scheduled while I was away on holiday and I was unable to attend. There was only the briefest mention of the ring in the local newspaper, which only gave the name of the parish as the findspot and I eventually received a half share in the £3750 award.

A year (almost to the day) after finding the medieval ring, I found a Roman silver ring with a gold stud supposedly representing the evil eye to protect the wearer. I reported to the Coroner and deposited it, in exchange for a Treasure Receipt, at a different museum which was more convenient at the time. The ring was disclaimed and returned to me with the landowner's agreement.

My next treasure find was the gold sixth century Saxon pendant (shown on page 32), which I reported to the same lady Coroner as the previous two finds. By this time the County Finds Liaison Officer (FLO) had taken over the role of 'treasure receiver' as a natural extension of his administration of the Portable Antiquities Scheme, where found objects are voluntary reported for inclusion on a national finds database. I handed over the pendant to the FLO in exchange for a Treasure Receipt. The local museum wished to acquire the find so it went to inquest, which I was able to attend, where the Coroner cautioned me not to give out the findspot in court! The press were present and interviewed me after the short hearing, later publishing a small article, only revealing the name of the parish, and a photograph of the pendant, which I had given them. I later received my share of the £1300 award.

My last potential treasure find to date is a seventeenth century gold posy ring, unfortunately badly damaged by agricultural machinery. I reported this to the same Coroner as previously and handed it over to the FLO in exchange for a Treasure Receipt. Not surprisingly it has been disclaimed.

Clearly there has been a vast improvement in the handling of potential treasure in my area over the past few years, however I still urge you to be cautious when reporting your finds. Here's my unofficial suggestions for protecting yourself and your landowner friends when you find potential treasure:

- Leave your find 'as found' and resist all temptation to clean or restore your find except for the absolute minimum necessary to identify it as possible treasure.
- The National Council for Metal Detecting will willingly advise in the process of reporting treasure and it is well worth involving them from the start when you have possible treasure to report.
- County Finds Liaison Officers (FLOs) are now heavily involved in the treasure process and will also advise and help.
- **Your only legal obligation is to report the finding of potential treasure to the Coroner within fourteen days of becoming aware that it is possibly treasure.**
- Discuss the matter with the landowner as soon as possible.
- Do the reporting yourself. The legal responsibility for reporting rests with the finder and no one will look after your interests as well as you.
- Bear in mind, especially if you want to keep the coin, that the first coin found of a scattered hoard may not be treasure, if it was the only coin found on that occasion and there was sufficient time to sell the coin before the finding of the second coin.
- Report your find to the Coroner in writing within 14 days and keep a copy of the letter. In the first instance only report the findspot as the name of the parish in which the find was made. If it is not clear which Coroner needs to be informed, ask your FLO or write to the most likely Coroner and ask for your letter to be passed on, as necessary.
- Always take photographs or have photographs taken of all possible views of all objects, before you hand the objects over. You will at least have something to show an independent valuer and, if you want to publish, you won't get stung with hefty copyright fees.
- There is no time limit for handing over the find and you should be allowed a reasonable amount of time for such things as photographing, valuing, showing it to the landowner, displaying it at a club meeting etc. Bear in mind, however, that you are responsible for the security of the find until you hand it over.
- You will probably be asked to hand your find over to a museum or the county Finds Liaison Officer, at your own expense. If you can arrange this without too much inconvenience then in the interest of good relationships it is best to comply. However, you are under no legal obligation to take your find anywhere and perfectly within your rights to politely suggest the Coroner arrange collection from you. FLOs often collect treasure objects from finders anyway.
- **Insist on being given the Treasure Receipt, (filled out in your presence) in exchange for your find.**

- The Treasure Act Code of Practice requires that the precise find spot must be established and should be kept confidential. You can insist on the confidentiality requirement when the Treasure Receipt is completed and have the precise findspot kept separately.
- A section of the Treasure Receipt is labelled "Location of findspot". Only enter vague details of the findspot such as name of Parish, four-figure map reference or a nondescript name for the site such as 'Field A'.
- If a museum is interested in acquiring the find, a Coroner's Inquest will be arranged. You should be invited to attend the Inquest for which you can claim expenses and I suggest you should attend if you possibly can – you will at least know who was there and what was said. The press may be there, so be careful not to reveal findspot information if they are.
- Following an Inquest the Press will probably want to speak to you. Whether you speak to them is up to you but you can at least appeal for some confidentiality and perhaps avoid them uncovering, or inventing, more than you would like revealed.
- The final stumbling block is the valuation, which will be given via the Department for Culture Media and Sport some weeks after the Inquest. You need to know if the valuation given is indeed 'A Fair Market Value' so that you can decide whether to accept it. Fair market value is an attempt to arrive at the price you should expect to get if selling your find on the open market and the Treasure Valuation Committee tries to arrive at the 'hammer' price without auctioneers deductions. Pick out a couple of dealers specialising in coins or objects similar to yours from the advertisements in the metal detecting press. Ask the dealers to give you their buying-in price for your find (you'll probably have to send photographs). I am sure they will oblige for little or no charge (say £5-£10 unless there is a lot of work involved or the treasure is very valuable). You will find that they will only give you a ballpark figure without seeing the actual finds, which you don't have. If the treasure is very rare it should be possible to arrange viewing for independent appraisal. You should be offered two opportunities to contest the valuation, one before the valuation committee meets and one after. I would accept the valuation if it falls within or above your dealers' ballpark figures and contest it if it falls below. If you are going to contest the valuation, get in before the committee meets if you can. There is a slight possibility that the museum involved may contest the valuation and succeed in getting it reduced – if this happens, unless there is clear justification, you could appeal against it all the way to the Secretary of State, if necessary.
- An alternative, if both you and the landowner agree, is to refuse any award for the find when you first report it, which will result in the find being disclaimed without inquest and valuation. You are unlikely to have the find returned, it will probably be taken by a museum.

Official Treasure Receipt (on two pages)

There are now two versions of the Treasure Receipt but the content is virtually identical and most importantly both are headed **Treasure Act 1996**. On the next page is the text from the 2003 version. The actual form can be downloaded from the Cultural Property page at: www.culture.gov.uk

Department for Culture, Media and Sport
Treasure Act 1996
Receipt for object(s)of potential treasure reported to the coroner
(Copies to be given to the depositor, the coroner and any body to which the object(s) are transferred. If the coroner has already been notified, please attach a copy of his acknowledgement. The SMR should also be informed of the find as soon as possible. The information concerning the findspot should normally be regarded as confidential.)
Reference no:
Institution receiving find:
Name of person receiving find: Tel:

Signature: Date:
Name of person examining find (if different):   Tel:
Signature of depositor: Date:
I confirm that the information given below concerning my name and address and the location, date and circumstances of the find is correct.
Reported to HM Coroner for the District of: Date:
Finder (1)   Name:
                            Address: Tel:
Finder (2)   Name:
                            Address: Tel:
(N.B. If there are more than two finders their names, addresses and telephone numbers should be noted separately. If the objects found by the different finders are to be kept separate, it might be better to fill out a separate form for each finder.)
Occupier of land   Name:
                            Address: Tel:
Owner of land   Name:
(if known and if   Address: Tel:
different from the occupier)
Date of find:
Circumstances of find:
(For example: depth of the find; whether on cultivated land or grassland; whether other objects, such as metal or pottery fragments or building rubble, have been found nearby. Continue on a separate sheet if necessary.)
Location of findspot:
(At least a six figure grid reference, along with the parish and county. A map may be attached. Since this information will be confidential, it may be advisable to keep a separate record of it.)
To be known as:
Brief description of object(s):
(For example: object type and material; Inscriptions or decoration; weight and dimensions; condition. A photograph may be included. Continue on a separate sheet if necessary.)
No. of items deposited:
Subsequent action –Subsequent transfers of the object(s) should be noted below
Institution receiving find:
Name of person receiving find: Tel:
Signature: Date:
Name of person examining find (if different):   Tel:
If object(s) are considered to be treasure, once the coroner has been informed, the British Museum/National Museums &Galleries of Wales should be notified.
Date of notification of British Museum/National Museums &Galleries of Wales:
If object(s)are not considered to be treasure, the coroner should be informed and authorisation sought to return the object(s):
Date of notification of coroner:
Date authorisation received from coroner:
Date of return of object(s):
Signature of recipient:
To download extra copies of this form, please visit the Cultural Property page at www.culture.gov.uk

LONG-RANGE LOCATORS

In the last ten years or so a number of devices known as Long-Range Locators (LRLs) have come onto the market. The manufacturers claim that Long-Range Locators will find gold and silver, find it deep, find it fast and find it from a mile or more away. Some, such as Electroscope and Lectrasearch, look like a fancy dowsing rod with an 'electronic' control box. They do not come cheap, being typically priced about equivalent to top of the range conventional metal detectors. With a conventional metal detector you can almost invariably locate the source of any signal, with a LRL you may or may not locate the source of any signal. This factor, coupled with claims of irrelevant circuit wiring and negligible battery power drain, has lead to much controversy and claims that these devices are a scam!

First let me say that if you study this book and put some of the ideas into practice – YOU WILL NOT NEED A LONG-RANGE LOCATOR – you will easily **out-perform** LRLs. However, from my own experience with an Electroscope Model 20, they do work and I believe the majority are basically dowsing devices which genuinely attempt to take the burden of discrimination away from the dowser. Yes, the circuit wiring may appear to be irrelevant but if no one knows how dowsing works, who can say what is irrelevant? Yes, battery drain may be negligible but I can remember receiving radio broadcasts on a crystal set with no battery whatsoever and when I switch my LRL on it works in a much more controlled manner than if I try and use it switched off.

Let me say again that dowsers have no real need for Long-Range Locators, (I very rarely use mine) however, if you already have one or are just plain interested, I will send you a **free** report on how you can use a Long-Range Locator (particularly the Electroscope M20) to find treasure. Just contact: David Villanueva, 43 Sandpiper Road, Whitstable, Kent, CT5 4DP or email david@truetreasurebooks.com/

BIBLIOGRAPHY AND FURTHER INFORMATION

Castle, J., *Hunting for Treasure*

Cox, Bill, *The Psychology of Treasure Dowsing*, (Santa Barbara, California, 1989)

Cross, Brian, J., *Another 1000 Roman Sites*, (Runcorn)

Cross, Brian, J., *Fair Sites of England*, (Runcorn, 1992)

Cross, Brian, J., *Fair Sites of Scotland*, (Runcorn)

Cross, Brian, J., *Finding Hammered Silver Coinage in England, Scotland and Wales*, (Runcorn, 1989)

Cross, Brian J., *More than 1000 Roman Sites*, (Runcorn)

Cross, Brian J., *Simple Site Research for Serious Detector Users*, (Runcorn, 1989)

Davies, Rodney, *Dowsing*, (Aquarian Press, London, 1991)

DCMS, *The Treasure Act 1996, Code of Practice (Revised), (England and Wales)*, (Department for Culture, Media and Sport 2-4 Cockspur Street, London SW1Y 5DH, 2002)

Fairley, John & Welfare, Simon, 'Water, Water, Everywhere', in *Arthur C Clarke's World of Strange Powers*, (London, 1984)

Field, John, *English Field Names: A Dictionary*, (Gloucester, 1989)

Fletcher, Edward, *A Treasure Hunter's Guide*, (Poole, 1975)

Fletcher, Edward, *Buried British Treasure Hoards and how to find them*, (Greenlight Publishing, 1996)

Fletcher, Edward, *Never Take No Fieldwalking as the Answer*, (Anglia Shoe Box Library)

Fletcher, Edward, *Please May I Fieldwalk on Your Farm*, (Anglia Shoe Box Library)

Fletcher, Edward *The Permission Producer*, (Anglia Shoe Box Library)

Fletcher, Edward, *Treasure Hunting for All*, (London, 1973)

Fletcher, Edward, *Your Quests For Anglo-Saxon Coins and Artefacts: How to do Better Next Time*, (Anglia Shoe Box Library, 1998)

Garrett, Charles L., *The Advanced Handbook on Modern Metal Detectors*, (Dallas, Texas, 1985)

Graves, Tom, *Discover Dowsing*, (Aquarian Press, London, 1989)

Graves, Tom, *The Dowser's Workbook*, (Aquarian Press, London, 1989)

Matacia, Louis J., *Finding Treasure Auras by Combining Science and Parapsychology*, (Bluemont, Virginia, 1996)

Matacia, Louis J., *Finding Treasure Combining Science and Parapsychology*, (Bluemont, Virginia, 1997)

Morris, John, Ed., *Domesday Book*, (Phillimore)

Naylor, P, *Discover Dowsing and Divining*, (Shire Publications, 1991)

Nielsen, Greg & Polansky, Joseph, *Pendulum Power*, (Aquarian Press, London, 1986)

Palmer, Andrew, *The Metal Detector Book*, (London, 1995)

Pickford, Nigel, *The Atlas of Shipwreck & Treasure*, (Dorling Kindersley, 1995)

Potter, John S. *The Treasure Diver's Guide*, (London, 1973)

Scott Elliot, J, *Dowsing: One Man's Way*, (British Society of Dowsers, 1996)

Selkirk, Raymond, *On the Trail of the Legions*, (Ipswich, 1995)

Short, Jeff, *County by County Guide to Treasure Hunting Sites*, (Brentwood, 1979)

Stine, G Harry, *Amazing and Wonderful Mind Machines You Can Build*, (Largo, Florida, 1997)

Welton, Thomas, *Jacob's Rod*, (London, 1874)

Wright, John, *Encyclopedia of Sunken Treasure*, (London, 1995)

Dowsing Societies

American Society of Dowsers, Inc. PO Box 24, Danville, Vermont 05828
Web: www.dowsers.org
The British Society of Dowsers, National Dowsing Centre, 2 St Ann's Road, Malvern, Worcestershire, WR14 4RG
Tel/Fax: 01684 576969
Web: www.britishdowsers.org
Canadian Society of Dowsers, 7-800 Queenstown Road, Suite 152, Stoney Creek, ON L8G 1A7   Tel: 1-888-588-8958
Web: www.canadiandowsers.org

Magazines

Lost Treasure, Box 451589, Grove, OK 74345-1589, USA   Tel: (800) 423-0029
Web: www.losttreasure.com
The Searcher, Searcher Publications, 17 Down Road, Merrow, Guildford, Surrey, GU1 2PX   Tel: 01483 830133
Web: www.thesearcher.co.uk
Treasure Hunting, Greenlight Publishing, The Publishing House, 119 Newland Street, Witham, Essex CM8 1WF
Tel: 01376 521900
Web: www.treasurehunting.co.uk
Western & Eastern Treasures, People's Publishing, PO Box 219, San Anselmo, CA 94979 Web: www.treasurenet.com/westeast

Metal Detecting Organisations

The National Council For Metal Detecting, General Secretary, 51 Hilltop Gardens, Denaby, Doncaster, DN12 4SA
Tel: 01709 868521   Web: www.ncmd.co.uk
The Federation Of Independent Detectorists, Colin Hanson, Detector Lodge, 44 Heol Dulais, Birchgrove, Swansea, West Glamorgan, SA7 9LT
Web: http://fid.newbury.net

Metal Detectors and Accessories

C.Scope, Kingsnorth Technology Park, Wotton Road, Ashford, Kent, TN23 6LN   Tel: 01233 629181
Web: www.cscope.co.uk
Crawfords Metal Detectors, Ninth Avenue, Flixborough Industrial Estate, North Lincolnshire, DN15 8SL   Tel: 01724 280993
Web: crawfordsmd.co.uk
Detecnicks, 3 Orchard Crescent, Arundel Road, Fontwell, West Sussex, BN18 0SD
Tel: 01243 545060
Web: www.detecnicks.co.uk

Garrett Metal Detectors, 1881 West State Street, Garland, Texas, 75042-6797 USA
Tel: 972-494-6151   Web: www.garrett.com
Joan Allen Electronics Ltd. 190 Main Road, Biggin Hill, Kent, TN16 3BB
Tel: 01959571255 Web: www.joanallen.co.uk
Kellyco, 1085 Belle Ave, Winter Springs, Florida 32708 Tel: 1-800-898-6673
Web: www.kellycodetectors.com
Maz Detecting Supplies, 100 Ynyshir Road, Mid Glamorgan, CF39 0EN
Tel: 01443 685336
Mike Longfield Detectors, 83 Station Road, Balsall Common, Nr Coventry, CV7 7FN   Tel: 01676 533274
Web: www.metaldetectors.gbr.cc
Minelab International Limited, Laragh, Brandon, Co. Cork, Ireland
Tel: 003532352102   Web: www.minelab.com
Old Maps   Web: www.old-maps.co.uk
Regton, 82 Cleveland Street, Birmingham, B19 3SN   Tel: 0121 359 2379
Web: www.regton.com
Spin-A-Disc Promotions, 107 Keighley Road, Illingworth, Halifax, HX2 8JE
Tel: 01422 245401
Web: www.metaldetectingbooks.co.uk
Viking Metal Detectors, 1 Angela Street, Mill Hill, Blackburn, BB2 4DJ
Tel: 01254 55887
Web: www.metaldetectors.co.uk
Whites Electronics (UK) Ltd, 35J Harbour Road, Inverness, IV1 1UA
Tel: 01463 223456   Web: www.whites.co.uk
World Treasure Books, PO Box 5, Newport, Isle of Wight, PO30 5QE   Tel: 01983 525169

Internet News Groups Etc.

alt.treasure.hunting
uk.rec.metaldetecting
www.smartgroups.com/groups/detecting
www.treasurenet.com
www.ukdetectornet.co.uk